D0747242

Swanee's Silverton

A firsthand account of
SILVERTON, COLORADO
from the 1930s to the Millennium

Gerald Swanson
AS TOLD TO KATHRYN RETZLER

WESTERN REFLECTIONS PUBLISHING COMPANY

Copyright © 2003 by Gerald Swanson
All Rights Reserved

No part of this book may be reproduced, for any reason, by any means, including any method of photographic reproduction, without the permission of the publisher.

Library of Congress Catalog Card Number: 2003104819
ISBN: 1-890437-94-8

Western Reflections Publishing Company
219 Main Street, Montrose, Colorado 81401
www.westernreflectionspub.com
westref@montrose.net

Book and jacket design, Kathryn Retzler, Ridgway, Colorado.

Swanee's Silverton

A firsthand account of

SILVERTON, COLORADO

from the 1930s to the Millennium

A special thank you to Kathryn Retzler,
for making this book happen and for all the hours we've spent together,
and to James Burke for his moral support.
You guys were great!

Swanee's Silverton

James Burke ©2002

✒ Silverton, Colorado. 2002 & 1898 ✒

Kathryn Retzler ©2002

Above, Swanee's Silverton today. The Grand Imperial hotel is on the left, the Benson Building (now home to Citizen's State Bank) on the right. Most of the buildings shown on the adjacent page are still there and still in use today.

Below, Silverton in 1898, about the time this story begins with the arrival of my grandparents, John and Dominica Dalla, in the late 1800s. The Teller Building (Teller House hotel today) is on the left, next to the Livery.

San Juan County Historical Society

❧ Silverton, Colorado. Circa 1940 ❧

Sandborn photo. San Juan County Historical Society

This is Swanee's Silverton at the end of the depression (and before World War II). Note the main street (Greene Street) is not paved. On the left, south of the Grand Hotel, the corner building (Iron Horse Indian Store today) is Tony Giacomelli's Bar. Tony was one of the town's finest accordion players. North of the Grand Hotel is the Blue Cross Drug Store, owned by Joe and Marie Dresback. They featured a Lucky Monday Sundae in a tall, fluted green glass with a scoop of vanilla and strawberry ice cream with chocolate and carmel sauce and nuts sprinkled on top. It cost fifteen cents and was served only on Monday. The Teen Center, in the basement, featured a lot of hand-painted murals done by local high school student Rudy Pozzatti, who went on to become a famous contemporary painter and head of the art department at Indiana University. The next building to the north (Fetch's, today) was the Club Cafe and Bar run by Bill and Svea Mowat. They did a little gambling in the basement those days—it was a cloak and dagger gambling operation. Some of that stuff is still in Fetch's basement. North of the Club Cafe was the Best Cafe, run by Buddy Lawrence and later on, the Fiore Giacomelli family.

South of Tony's Bar, the building with the paned windows, was Crippled Mary's liquor store. In front of that (foreground, left) was the San Juan Grocery & Market, run by Silverton mayor, Johnny Foreman. Looking north, you can see the old Lode Theater marquee.

On the right, at the Texaco sign, is the Circle Route Garage owned by L.W. Purcell. He served as chairman of the Democratic party in Silverton for forty years and also had the Silverton franchise to provide power from Western Colorado Power Company. What is now Henry Smith's Gifts was the coal storage. Just this side of it (out of sight here) was Mrs. Closter's wallpaper store in the old livery building. ✳

✍ Introduction ✍

One of the first things you notice in Gerald Swanson's recollections is the incredible ingenuity displayed by Gerald and his friends when he was growing up. The world may have been in a depression—Gerald was born in 1930—or at war, but Gerald and his buddies didn't let that stop them from having fun. They made skis out of barrel slats, swimming holes out of effluent water, spending money from junk sales. They sailed homemade boats down Greene Street's spring runoff and played street games like Kick-the-Can and touch football.

Their pranks were legendary—once the kids put a donkey up on the school-house roof. They played hard and worked hard—after-school chores were a part of life. Gerald and his friends shared a wonderful camaraderie that TV-watching, latchkey kids today will never experience.

"Nobody had to worry about entertaining us, about giving us the latest electronic gadgets," Gerald says. "We always had plenty to do."

He vividly remembers the days when the town still had a viable economic base, based on mining rather than tourism, and how he and his friends made the most of it. "We ran errands for the shady ladies of Blair Street, collected bottles and junk during the depression and sold it for pocket money to spend at Giacomelli's Confectionery" (now the Pickle Barrel). Gerald and his friends also pinched neighborhood chickens for illegal barbecuing down by Cement Creek, "borrowed" sheepherders' donkeys for impromptu backyard rodeos and tipped a few occupied outhouses. In teenage years, they'd sit on the curb (before the 9 p.m. curfew), in front of the Benson or Club bar, listening to the piano player and "hopin' there'd be a good bar fight."

One boyhood chore involved milking cows kept in the barn all winter. Gerald recites how the dairyman, after over-indulging at a local establishment, "came home plastered, slipped in the knee-high mixture of muck and snow, blamed the cows and punched one on the noggin, knocking it flat."

Then there was the matter of Mrs. Mattivi's goats. "She lived across the street (from the Swanson Market, Gerald's home and now the Dallavalle Inn). Her goats climbed up on top of Sheriff Patterson's new Terraplane convertible car. They fell clean through to the seats, ripping open the soft top. The sheriff hauled Mrs. Mattivi down to the jail!"

Gerald's memory is prodigious. He can and does recite the class roster, including the teachers and members of the basketball teams from every year he attended the Silverton school. He kept scrapbooks and took photos, and kept track over the years of the people in this remarkable town where he eventually held jobs from meatcutter to mayor...and more.

Through it all, he remained a consummate storyteller.

After college and a stint in Korea, Gerald settled into town politics and worked alongside his mother, Mary, at Swanson's Market. But not before a few adventurous jobs around town. He briefly tended bar at his uncle's Columbine Tavern and recalls "when old Doc Holt's girlfriend dropped her new fur coat and was totally naked underneath except for her spiked high heels!"

Working at the family market, he recalls one incident where he had sold some meat "to old Ben Bagozzi, who made a stew of it then blew it all over his cabin and himself and clean out the front door. After which he returned what was left of his pressure cooker to Carl D. Curtis Hardware because it 'didn't work.'"

Like his mother, Gerald dispensed over the grocery counter equal amounts of news and groceries for more than forty years. From the front window of Swanson's Market, he and his mother Mary watched Hollywood movies being filmed. He watched, with an occasional jaundiced eye, fistfights and gunfights (real and pretend) taking place on the town's notorious Blair Street.

Through it all he saw Silverton prosper and struggle, boom and bust. Over and over again.

But, simply a sitter and watcher Gerald wasn't. He got involved. He helped bring back the popular hardrock mining contests, led Fourth of July parades (decked out in an incredible array of costumes), brought television to town, performed in local theater productions and more than once helped Chief of Police Art Weibe roust a well-oiled citizen from where he was sleeping in his car behind the Benson Hotel. Gerald served as mayor and Republican County Chairman, training under Art Lorenzon, who ran the old Post Office Drugstore. "I learned politics from him. Old Art kept separate cash registers for every section of his drug store, which is sort of how he ran this town, too."

This, then (and now), is Swanee's Silverton: Gerald Swanson's story of a unique mountain town, told from his own unique perspective. No hard-core, cut and dried historical account, this is one man's compelling, entertaining, personal account of the people and the town where he has spent his entire life.

Swanee's Silverton is a tale worth telling.

And, it is a tale worth preserving.

Kathryn Retzler

✂ One ✂

Dalla Boarding House

We lived over there in the old Dalla Boarding House on Cement Street, next to Cement Creek. It was a twenty-room, two-story, frame building. It had a bar room twenty-five by fifty feet, with a back bar and a front bar, and behind it, a big common room. There was a boardinghouse-style kitchen, with a huge coal-fired range, about twelve feet long, built of cast iron and steel. You had to have room for a lot of pots to cook for all the boarders. My grandparents, John and Domenica Dalla, who ran it before I came along, also had eleven children, including Mary, my mother. All together, they took up a lot of space! They fixed two or three meals a day. They had kitchen help and two big sinks, one to wash, one to rinse. And a drainboard to put the dishes on until they were fairly dry. In the morning, there would be a big kettle of coffee on the iron coal range, and another bucket of hot milk. Sometimes the old-timers, especially the Italian miners, would throw a couple of eggs in the milk and dip bread in it.

Behind the kitchen, on one side, was a small group of bedrooms. Attached to the kitchen was a lean-to, a kind of add-on building with a galvanized metal bathtub—the only one for the entire building.

The Dalla family. My grandmother, Domenica, holding my mother Mary, left. My grandfather John, seated on right, died of frostbite in 1911 when he was just fifty years old, leaving Domenica with nine children to raise and a boardinghouse to run. She died seven years later, along with two of her sons, in the influenza epidemic.
Gerald Swanson collection

People didn't take too many baths in those days, usually just on Saturday, although we always had to wash our face, hands and feet before going to bed. And, my mother always inspected our ears to make sure we'd washed them out.

Thundermugs & outhouses

There was only one toilet, a one-holer, downstairs on the bottom floor. The sewer ran directly into Cement Creek. Out back there was a four-holer outhouse, which most of the boarders used—along with tons of old catalogs and newspapers. Even though we poured lime down there once a week, you could never cut down on the number of flies in the summer. And if the roof leaked, you could never cut down on the icicles around the hole. The bedrooms all had thundermugs, just as a precaution (which was a good thing, because in the

1917. Herman Dalla, at Frasher's Pond, base of Kendall Mountain.

Gerald Swanson collection

winter it was too cold to get out of a warm bed with a down mattress and go out to the outhouse). The boarders had to dump their own thundermugs, but the hired gals, who cleaned the rooms and changed the linens once a week, went around every day to make sure they did.

Wash days

Washing linens and clothes in those days was not easy. Mary and her mother (my grandmother Domenica) washed everything by hand, using washboards and lye soap and heating the water on the old coal-fueled range.

They hung the sheets out early in the morning, so they could bring them in by 10 a.m. before the trains came.

1919. Fury, Louis, Mary and Angelo Dalla, in front of Dalla Boarding House. Mary was just 16, and had to quit school to run the boardinghouse and care for the family.

Gerald Swanson collection

The trains went right past the back door. In the winter, they hung the laundry all over the kitchen, then stoked up the range.

Those old coal-fueled stoves were pretty handy. They did everything—you could dry clothes, bake, heat water and heat the house with one of those old stoves. The City Hall, County Court House, Hospital and Miner's Union all had coal-fired steam heat. The American Legion still heats by coal today.

Mary Dalla (center) with the Anesi sisters, Louisa (left) and Annie. Little girl in front is Lydia Antonelli (daughter of Mary's sister, Rena).
Gerald Swanson collection

Food storage & preservation

The boardinghouse also had a big basement, where we stored dry goods, groceries, sacks of flour and sugar, all put in old metal cans so the mice wouldn't get them. Vegetables were stored down there in cool sand, in sand bins. We didn't have any fresh produce in the winter. Instead, there was lots of cabbage, turnips, carrots, onions, potatoes and beets, things that could be stored in the cool basement. We did a lot of home canning, too. Fruit, like apricots, pears and apples were usually dried, then reconstituted, especially for pies. There were smoked meats and fish, even trout. And beef jerky. We kept pickles down there, too, in big barrels. And sauerkraut. Some of the old miners would drink the juice.

The old-time freezers were big, monstrous iceboxes. There was an ice pond north of Silverton. Once a week they'd go up there and cut ice, then bring it into town and store it in the top of the iceboxes. The melting ice would drain down into the sewers or be piped into storage barrels. The system kept things cool enough they didn't rot, but not cold like today.

Everybody learned to preserve and prepare for the winter. We used everything. There wasn't any waste, any garbage disposals. We used it all. Mutton fat, for instance, was used to waterproof boots. Old clothes were mended until they were no more than rags, then they were used as rags. Old reading material went to the outhouse. Uneaten food went to the poor.

1932. Julia Maffey, Rosie Andreatta, Irwin Swanson, Letizia Maffey in front of the French Bakery.

Gerald Swanson collection

Prohibition & the revenuers

My mother, who ran the boardinghouse after her mother died of the influenza in 1918, told a story about a guy named Poncha who helped in the kitchen. Now, this was during Prohibition, which started in 1918, but in Colorado started four years earlier. There was a saloon at the boardinghouse in those days, and old Poncha, he liked to drink, but not at the bar. Turns out, he was doing his drinking in the pantry. My mother would send him there to get some flour or sugar, and he'd be taking a long-time. She'd yell at him to hurry up, then she found he was back there drinking vanilla. It had a twelve percent alcohol content. No wonder they were always running out of vanilla!

Everybody made wine, whiskey, brandy and beer at home, even before Prohibition. There was always something to drink in the kitchen. Italians in particular had wine in the kitchen. And, they always made homemade root beer for us kids.

During Prohibition, there was some violence here, according to stories told by city council men who were bootleggers. They worked closely with the revenuers (agents) to blow the whistle on any competition in town, so the revenuers wouldn't destroy the booze, but confiscate it and bring it to those same council men, who would then buy it back from the revenuers. There were a lot of under-the-table deals going on.

My mother told the story about the best way to handle revenuers. Somebody in Durango would call the depot in Silverton and warn when revenuers were riding up on the train. Everybody would ditch their booze.

1920. Angelo and Mary Dalla at the Dalla Boarding House

Gerald Swanson collection

The revenuers would come up, inspect the saloons and bars, but they wouldn't find anything. One time the booze got dumped in a pasture. The cows were drunk for a week!

John and Domenica Dalla and their son Joseph immigrated from the Tyrol in the late 1800s.

Gerald Swanson collection

One day, two revenuers came to inspect the Dalla Boarding House. When my Uncle Angelo Dalla lifted the basement door so they could see what was down there, one of them accidentally dropped the .45 (caliber gun) he was holding. It went off, and the bullet went through the floor next to my mom. Uncle Angelo lifted that revenuer by the collar and threw him out in the snow.

"Don't you ever come back here again, or I'll press charges." Uncle Angelo shouted. He also threatened to kill him if he did.

That revenuer never did come back.

The Dalla family

There were a lot of Italian families here around the time my grandfather built the boarding-house. Many of them came from the Tyrol, an area in south Austria that later became part of Italy. Local newspapers there had advertised that there was work in the mines in the San Juans. Many of the men, including my grandfather, immigrated here.

My grandmother and their first son Joseph, who had been born in the Tyrol, followed later. They all became American citizens in 1900 and

Mary Dalla was 16 when her mother died, leaving her to care for her siblings and run the boardinghouse.

Gerald Swanson collection

were involved in a number of businesses including the boardinghouse and saloon, a bottling works, wholesale liquor and a farm in Mancos. He and Domenica had ten more children. Two, Charlie #1 and Charlie #2 both died when they were babies. Charlie was not a lucky name for the Dallas.

John Dalla died when he was just fifty years old. Just eleven years after he became a citizen and Americanized his name from Giovanni Dallavalle to John Dalla. He was trailing a small herd of cattle up from the family farm in Mancos and came across two cattle drivers. It was late fall, and they were caught in a sudden, early blizzard. My grandfather might have made it, but when he tried to help his two companions

Mary Dalla, Mary Tomaselli, Eda Ellis, in front of the Dalla Boarding House.

Gerald Swanson collection

Angelo Dalla's taxi, before and after it took a spill in Telluride. That's Angelo at the wheel, and checking the wreck on the right.

Gerald Swanson collection

through the storm, he wound up getting frostbite. Back in Silverton, he had to have his leg amputated (from the frostbite), then died of pneumonia. (One of the drivers died too; the other survived.) My grandfather's death was a real tragedy; he was a very strong man. My mother told a story how he could lift a fifty-gallon cask of wine from a buckboard, or get under a pool table, with four men on the pockets, and lift it a few inches off the floor, just with his back!

After he was gone, Domenica, who could barely speak English and was pregnant with [my Uncle] Herman and had a hard time of it. My mother said that there

were years when Domenica never even made it the few blocks over to town, because there was so much work to do. Then my grandmother died too, along with two of her sons, all of them victims of the 1918 influenza epidemic.

My mother, Mary, was sixteen at the time. She had to quit school to take care of the family and the boardinghouse, with some help from her sister Rena. But Rena left when she was fourteen to marry Fidenzio (Phil) Antonelli. They moved over to Blair Street where the Dalla family had another boardinghouse and saloon (present-day Dallavalle Inn).

Top: My parents, Mary and Irwin Swanson with me at Grandma Swanson's house in Durango.

Right: With my sister Jean and my mother in Silverton.

Both photos,
Gerald Swanson collection

Mary's brother, Angelo, operated the Day and Night Taxi Service out of Silverton. Aunt Rena told the story about how, in 1927, they took four Swedish miners to Denver via Red Mountain Pass. The road was rudimentary at best. They met another car on the one-lane road and got to arguing with the driver who should go first. Meanwhile, the powerful Swedes lifted the other car off the road. And, they were on their way!

Mary Dalla married my father, Irwin Swanson, while she was still in the old Dalla Boarding House. I came along in 1930. I was a preemie,'born at the hospital in Montrose, and weighed just three and three-quarter pounds. My mother brought me home on a pillow and fed me with an eye dropper. I slept in the top drawer of the dresser, with a light bulb to keep me warm. It was a homemade incubator.

And, would you believe, after seventy-two years, I grew to be a strapping 230 pounds!

My sister Jean was born two years later. We lived at the boardinghouse until 1938, when we moved to the building on Blair Street.

The Dalla Boarding House burned to the ground in the early 1970s. It had been sold twice before that. There were some guys living there when it burned. They threw a big party, and one guy threw white gas instead of coal oil on the fire (a not uncommon occurrence, especially where alcohol was involved). As a result, one man burned to death. Another jumped off a balcony, but he lived. All that's left there now is an empty lot. ✳

1934. My fourth birthday party, Durango.
L-R, Rita Duran, Cynita Kiel, Gerald Swanson, Carl Longstrom, Lewis Oberrick (peeking out), Earl Barker (who owns Strater Hotel today), Donald Burnett, Julia Burrows.

Above, back row: Rita Doran, Cynita Kiel, Rudy Tipiotch, Donald Burnett, Lewis Oberrick, Carl Longstrom, Earl Barker.

Both photos,
Gerald Swanson collection

Two

School & Play Days

The school was (and still is) over on Reese Street. There weren't any school buses in those days and nobody's parents drove them. We walked. It wasn't too bad when the weather was good, but in the winter, we often had to wade through waist-high snow to get there. People were more prepared for the winters then, and I think there was a lot more snow. I remember it standing over three feet deep at the boardinghouse.

Back in the early thirties, we didn't have roads open year around, but the railroad was usually open. A railroad blockade, like the one in '32, didn't cause too much hardship, however, because people stored food in their basements. The big problem was hay to feed the milk cows. Even when the roads were open, freighting hay could be expensive. So, people cut the hay bales in half and mailed them up here. The mail was one of the first things to get through.

When I started school in 1936, there were twenty-nine kids in my first grade class. When I graduated there were still twenty kids, all of them born and raised in Silverton. The economy was more stable—it depended on the mines rather than

1939. Silverton School Gymnasium.   Gerald Swanson collection tourism. The big mines were all open, the Shenandoah Dives and Mayflower Mill, Pride of the West, Highland Mary, Idarado, the North Star and Sultan. Miners were taking silver, gold, lead, copper and zinc (all the base metals) out of these mountains.

"We were a real town then!"

There were four grocery stores, two drugstores, two complete hardware stores, two or three doctors and dentists. The optometrist would come to town and set up at the Imperial Hotel, where for a couple of days he would measure you for eye glasses right there. The Silverton Drygoods, just south of the Wyman Building, was run by Joe Chino. He carried a full line of shoes and work boots, suits, overalls, dress shirts

Circa 1939. My sister Jean and I (right) with our cousins Gladys and Phil Antonelli. In front of Swanson's Market, after the Swanson's moved to Blair Street.

Gerald Swanson collection

and ladies clothing. You didn't have to go down to Durango or Montrose to find what you needed. If you needed your shoes replaced or repaired, there was a cobbler where the Train Store is now. Grenache's Shoe Repair—he sold Red Wing shoes. And Tocco's Mercantile, right there on Blair (where the Candle Shop is now), carried everything too.

We didn't have so many clothes like we do today. Usually you had just two sets—one for dress up (like the miners' "go-to-town" suit), the other for school or work. And you were lucky if you had two pairs of shoes or boots. When they got

1935. With my sister Jean in front of the Dalla Boarding House with Lena Matties (of the Welcome Saloon, now Natalia's)

Gerald Swanson collection

worn out, you took them to the cobbler to be fixed. Today, people just throw things out and go to Wal-Mart to buy more!

Back to school

This was the chore we didn't like, because we all had to get our hair trimmed up, since we'd been running bald-headed all summer. (First thing we did in the summer, when school was out, was get our heads shaved so we didn't have to comb our hair. It was easier for swimming. You could just jump in the water and not worry about it!) In the fall, we had to get new shoes, usually too big, so you could grow into them during the school year. Most of them had thick rubber soles. Rubber lasted better than leather. You also got new bib overalls each fall—

Below: 1936-1937. My first grade class. Silverton Public School, (Note the boys in their bib overalls.)
Top row: Clee Robinson, Gerald Swanson, Henry Bogolino, Leroy Diller, James Sony Drobnick, Darrell Ferguson, Richard Ellis, (?), Donald Higman, Carl Peterson, Richard Maes, Clyde Todeschi, Buster Everett, George Salazar.
Bottom row: Carmen Romero, Eileen Ellis, Stela Quintana, Jackie McClary, Mary Moretti, Viola Atencio, Dorothy Knoll, Berlinda Atencio, Joann Ashenbrenner, Gladys Antonelli, Virginia Burton, Nancy Lund, Etta Knuckles, Helen Loback.

Collection of historical mementos from curio cabinet at Dallavalle Inn.

Gerald Swanson collection

because they were the easiest to handle. Our overalls were plain, not those fancy, striped engineer ones you can buy today. And our shirts were denim or wool, which were warm but scratchy as hell. By the end of the school year, both had a lot of patches, especially at the elbows and knees. The girls wore plain dresses. And stockings. My mother always used to put my poor sister in long, brown stockings. As soon as we got out of reach of the house, my sister would roll them down like anklets, because the girls didn't want to be caught wearing old brown stockings! Girls didn't wear pants then, like they do today.

So anyway, getting ready for school was a chore. You were expected to dress real good the first two days of school. The second day they always took class pictures. All the way through, from first grade on, they took the pictures the second day, before the kids' clothes were torn and patched, while they still looked their best. It made sense. You didn't wait six months to get your pictures, and then have to go out and buy new clothes. You did it to save money and save time and get the job done. So there everybody was in the picture, smiling, with a new haircut and new bib overalls.

As soon as you got home, you changed out of your good school clothes and put on your old, summertime play clothes. Of course, this didn't always happen right away. A lot of times, we'd stop to play. The streets were unpaved and full of rocks.

We'd be playing touch football, and kids would pick up the rocks and throw them at each other. We'd be falling down, ripping the knees out of our overalls, scuffing up our shoes and getting holes in them. I'd try to sneak past my mother and go up and change clothes, but she usually caught me.

Nobody had to entertain us

When the weather was warm, and even sometimes when it wasn't, we'd play in the streets, games like touch football, kick-the-can, run-sheep-run and pickup sticks. With that one, you had five or six guys on a side. You'd draw a line across the street and put out about ten to fifteen wood sticks. Then you'd go to war! Each side tried to prevent the other from picking up sticks. Guys got knocked down, some were crying, sticks were flyin' all over. It was a lot of fun, like a hockey game played in a dusty old street. You wore out your shoes and put holes in your overalls. We had a great time.

Kick-the-can, we played in the middle of an intersection on a side street, like Reese or Snowden. You put a guard there at the intersection, servicing two blocks. It was best played at night because they didn't have many streetlights. Just one on the corner. You'd try to

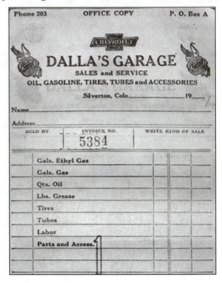

Top left, my sled when I was a boy. Above and left, sales and service tickets from the Dalla Garage on "main" street, owned by my uncle Angelo Dalla in the 1920s and 1930s.

Gerald Swanson collection

sneak into the perimeters where the other team's guard couldn't see you, and kick-the-can, while a couple of the other team's guys tried to harass you. The game goes on till everybody drops from exhaustion.

Run-sheep-run is like hide-and-seek. One team runs and hides, the other tries to find it.

We also played with BB guns, when we could get them, and when we were old enough. You'd wear a small mesh-wire mask, like a face shield, so we wouldn't get hit in the eye with a BB. The best place for that was an old mill or mine someplace like the North Star or Sultan Mill.

Another favorite game was King of the Hill. This one was played in the winter, when there were big piles of snow on the streets. You'd choose a side, you know, like drawing straws from an old broom. Four or five guys would get on one team, four or five on another. One team would climb on top of a snow pile, and the other one would try to drag them off. It could be a lot of fun, especially when big chunks of snow and ice would land on you and hit you in the head.

They won't let you do stuff like that today. Too dangerous. Better to sit on the couch and watch some violent TV show, where the guy getting hit on the head is only on a TV screen.

We didn't have too many organized sports in those days. I don't think the adults, even our parents, took the interest in play that they do today for our kids. Nobody had to entertain us or provide us with something to do. We found plenty to do ourselves, and we did it away from the adults as much as possible. As my old Swedish grandmother used to say, "You children are to be seen and not heard."

We had to figure out our own entertainment, and sometimes figuring out our own entertainment was not probably the best thing because we would hear our older peers and our uncles, tell us about what they used to do. And then we'd try to duplicate that, or better yet "one up" on them.

When we weren't out there terrorizing the streets, we might be saving up for a special treat. For my sister and I, and the guys I hung around with, a big treat was going to town to see a movie.

Movies, treats and sweets

The old Lode Theater (next to the corner where Hold your Horses is today) was owned by a guy named Dewey who also owned Lode Theaters in Ouray and Telluride. The movies changed three times a week, although we'd be lucky if we got to go once a month.

Lode Theater on Greene Street, fronted with high snow. This picture was taken in 1947, but the theater remained much unchanged for more than 20 years— except for the movies listed on the marquee. Left is the Post Office Drug Store, a favorite for treats.

Gerald Swanson collection

We'd save up for weeks and hope we didn't get in any kind of trouble in the meantime, so our mother wouldn't let us go. There was no such thing as being grounded back then, and they couldn't take a lot away from you because we didn't have a lot to be taken away. But they could take away your candy or your bicycle—well, we all didn't have bicycles. My sister and I shared one bicycle when I was in grade school. I could use it one day, and my sister could use it the other. So the threat of taking away or being grounded or time-out, never existed. You either got your butt swatted good or you got a real good dressing down or you didn't get out of the house. You went to school and came home. That was it.

There wasn't much to take away from you—your music or anything. And they couldn't threaten you by saying you can't go to the picture show because, hell, we could never go to the picture show much anyway—we didn't have the money. Even at ten cents a shot for the picture show, you didn't have the money. It didn't exist. One way we made money, though, enough for the picture show, was washing bottles. (Later during the war, we'd collect junk and sell it.)

Candy was another treat. We could never get enough of it. Where the Pickle Barrel is now, was Rosie Tinor's Giacomelli Confectionery. (See photos, next page.) It was a complete shopping area. On the left, as you came in, was a twelve-foot candy case, where all the kids in town went for candy. Next was an ice cream dipping station, then the 3.2 beer for kids eighteen and older. There was a step-up balcony where you could go to drink beer. On the other side of the room you could buy alcohol by the bottle, and there was also a mini gift store. Back in the kitchen, they sold homemade wine, and there were rooms for two or three 'scarlet ladies' of the 'lost generation.' From kids to adults, it was a one-stop shopping center.

They also had a number of pool halls in town that sold 3.2 beer. One of the finest pool halls was where the Handlebars is now. It had two bowling alleys, three billiard tables, 3.2 beer (for 18 and older) and the only popcorn in town. Beer was

Above: Rosie (Giacomelli) Tinor, left and her father with an employee in Giacomelli's Confectionery, which Mr. Tinor built in the late 1800s.

Below: Fiore (pronounced Fury) Giacomelli and Maggie, his wife at Giacomelli's forty years later, in the 1930s. Notice the slot machines on rolling carts. They could be hidden away when there was a raid. Movie star posters are up on the right. Kool Cigarettes cost fifteen cents. I had my first beer here, when I was eighteen, at the little bar upstairs (on the left). The stone building today is the Pickle Barrel, and is one of Silverton's oldest, still-used business establishments. The photograph above hangs in the small bar at the back of the Pickle Barrel.

Both photos, San Juan County Historical Society

Above: Louis and Herman Dalla standing on the county Quick Way Steam Shovel, late 1930s. It had a drag line, and was like an early caterpillar on tracks. Uncle Herman worked for the County Road Crew.

Below: Herman Dalla and Joe Todeschi on Molas Pass.

Both, Gerald Swanson collection

twenty cents a bottle. Popcorn was five cents a bag. When I got a little older, I used to set pins in the bowling alleys. We kids would hand set for a nickel a bowler. It cost a person twenty cents a game to bowl.

Sometimes we'd go over to Frecker's Confectionery. It was over in the Grand Hotel, where Ortegas has the Indian Store now, on the corner. At one time, that was the original Hub Saloon. He sold Big Chief tablets, pencils, magazines, ice cream and soda pop. He used to make ice cream sandwiches there. It cost five cents, the sandwich crust was made out of the cone, the ice cream was frozen in between. A bowl of ice cream cost a quarter, no matter what size the container.

Grade school

In 1936, I started the first grade. Mrs. McLaughlin was my first grade teacher. We didn't like her much. Mrs. Marshall was my second grade teacher. She was about six-two or six-three, with a honeycomb hairdo curled clear to the top of her head. The second day of class she sat us down and called out our names, "Gladys Antonelli, Viola Atencio, Henry Bogolino, Jimmy Drobnick, Helen Loback, Richard Maes, Mary Moretti, Lynn Murray, Carmen Romero, Joe Salazar, Gerald Swanson, Clyde Todeschi ... all you 'wop' and Mexican and other ethnic kids have to sit in the back two rows" she said. "You American kids sit up front."

There was a lot of ethnic prejudice against some of us kids then. When I got home, I asked my mother what a 'wop' was.

"Why?" she asked.

I told her what Mrs. Marshall had said in class. Now, my mother never went down to the school. She figured the teachers were always right. But this time, my mother marched right down there and went in to see Superintendent Brenton. When she told him what Mrs. Marshall had said, he went to the classroom, pulled Mrs. Marshall out and gave her a real dressing down.

"We won't have any of that ethnic segregation in our classrooms," he said.

Mrs. Marshall never did like me much after that.

My sixth grade teacher was Mrs. Brown. We used to sing about her when

Foresters of America Labor Day Celebration

Silverton, Colo., 1936

Two Days' Celebration
September 6 and 7.

Gerald Swanson collection

she couldn't hear us. "Mrs. Brown went to town with her pants hangin' down." The kids would shoot spitballs at her, too. When we got caught, she'd get out the paddle. But before she did, Mrs. Brown would call the janitor, John Benash, to witness the paddling. There were three holes in that paddle that created a kind of vacuum. So it was a double sting. Another of her favorite punishments was the dunce cap. It was a paper cone labeled "Dunce" and if you were bad, you had to wear it on your head and stand in the corner.

It's not like that now, is it?

Sheepherders' Days

One of the big events in town was Sheepherders' Days, held on Labor Day. There were all kinds of entertainments and contests, including mining contests, which were held right downtown. There was a carnival and contests for kids. My favorite was the pie eating contest. Whoever ate the most pie in the shortest time—without using their hands—won a silver dollar. That was a lot of money in those days.

They had "hokey" shows for the men. The ladies were billed as exotic dancers from the far east or the near east. They were belly dancers. There were "carny" dice and milk bottle throwing, a carousel and a Ferris wheel. They had this big cart with

Hardrock Mining Contests, held here on the corner of 12th and Greene in 1938, became a tradition during mining's heydays and have recently become popular again.

San Juan County Historical Society

a big fat cook making greasy hamburgers. A ten-cent hamburger and a glass of good, sharp lemonade was the best fare in town!

When the sheepmen came to town, it was quite a scene. All the dogs in town would be chasing the sheep, along with the sheep dogs. The herders would drive three or four thousand sheep right through town—you can imagine the dust and the noise and all that confusion. The old ladies on Blair Street would get out their brooms to keep the animals from running through their gardens. Dust would be flyin', flies would be buzzin' and dogs would be barking.

We kids loved it.

The herders—most of them were Basque (they say they're the best sheep-herders in the world)—would tie their horses and donkeys up behind the Benson Hotel and go into the saloon there, the County Club. ("County Club" is still carved into the fascia of the old building at the corner of 12th and Greene.)

Donkey rodeos

We boys would wait while the herders went in there and started drinking, then we'd steal their donkeys and put them in a barn or a shed up the street. Then we'd have donkey rodeos. There were five of us: Delmar Pratt, Gerald Dalla (no relation), Sammy

Kids' pie eating contest.
Gerald Swanson collection

Anesi Maynes (he's an attorney in Durango now; he was one of the best burrow riders), me and Alfonso Gallegos. They called Alfonso "Fatso the Bomber."

Fatso used to like to play with blasting caps. He'd put them on a railroad tie and hit them with a rock. One time he blew off two fingers and the tip of the thumb on his left hand when the blast split the rocks into shrapnel. Fatso was a tough little bugger.

Anyway, we'd keep the donkeys until one of the cops (Frank Salfisberg, Roy Roff or Frank Brown) would come down and say, "You boys got those donkeys in a shed up there? You take them back downtown now."

That's me with one of the donkeys like we boys used for burrow rodeos.

Gerald Swanson collection

While the carnival was going on, and we were having our donkey rodeos, the sheep were all kept in pens where the RV Park is now (at the southwest end of town). They'd stay there until they were calmed down, then go down to Durango on the train.

But the herders never got all of the sheep out of the hills. So after Labor Day, locals would go up in the hills looking for lost sheep. Nobody ever turned them in when they found them, although they were supposed to. Those sheep would make for a nice fat lamb chop or leg of lamb later on. One time the postmaster and the cousin of the president of the local fish and game club got caught with twelve illegal sheep stored in a pen near Cement Creek. They each got fined $5 for each sheep.

Sewer-water swimming

Summertime was the best time for playing. We had chores to do, of course, and summer jobs, but the rest of the time we were free to fish and hike and run around finding ways to get up to mischief—all the necessary things kids do who live in the mountains. Like swimming.

Swimming was one of our favorite activities. One of our best swimming holes, believe it or not—talk about a crazy bunch of kids—was down at the second bridge on the Animas River. There was a big, deep pool, and just about a quarter of a mile above that was where the sewer dumped in. (The city sewer used to dump raw sewage in the river: we didn't have a 'proper' sewer system until 1950). In any case, we were swimming in water downstream from where the sewer came in. Nobody got sick, but when you get to thinking about it, I'd of killed my kids today if they'd wanted to do those things. But what the heck, back then, we just did it. Nobody ever worried about it. And of course like I've said before, you just did things. Maybe they weren't the smartest things, and maybe we did things because we didn' know better, and maybe we did things because our parents or uncles did them before us. Whatever the reason, we all survived without any ill effects.

Summertime picnics

Another big summertime activity was hiking and picnicking. We had huge family picnics, usually at South Mineral or Minnie Gulch, and usually two or three times a year. The Dalla and Todeschi and Antonelli families all came, and often some of the Matties' and other Tyrolean families in town. It's a tradition that dates to the late 1800s. There would always be a keg of beer, two or three small kegs of homemade wine and jugs of Italian grappa, which was the Italian form of bootleg whiskey. They'd usually plug and spike a watermelon with the grappa, then cool it icy-cold in Mineral Creek.

South Mineral provided water for the town of Silverton. They had a water line out to it in those days. It was great drinking water. Great for fishing, too, and wading, always cold and crystal clear. And it was for the locals, not loaded up like it is today with tourists from Dallas, Tucumcari and Whatsit, Illinois.

Late 1950s. Above: Minnie Gulch (halfway between Howardsville and Eureka). Herman, Louis, Fury, Rena, Mary, Angelo and Joseph Dalla. This photo is the last of the nine living Dallas. Members of the Todeschi and Antonelli families came, too, and some of the Matties' and other Tyrolean families in town. The tradition carries back to late 1896.

Gerald Swanson collection

We never charcoaled things then. We had a little portable grill we'd bring out and light a fire underneath it. And big cast iron skillets for cooking steak, or chicken, pounded and sautéed in pure butter and garlic, served up on Italian hard buns with good, traditional pasta. Some folks brought Italian polenta, brown gravy and pork and beef stew. There was also homemade sauerkraut, apple strudel and lots of German/Austrian dishes as well as Italian.

Mary Swanson, Celia Todeschi Troglia (standing), Juanita "Teddie" Todeschi and John Troglia.
Gerald Swanson collection

These were people of the Tyrol, after all, people of both German and Italian ancestry. Then there were lots of desserts, homemade cakes, big, tall chocolate cakes with boiled white icing and coconut on top. I could never get enough of that. My aunt Lena Dalla (married to my Uncle Louis) and my cousin Celia Todeschi Troglia always brought the most wonderful desserts.

Playing boccie ball.
Gerald Swanson
collection

Men played boccie ball (an Italian form of lawn bowling), or, if they were too old, sat around and argued. The women crocheted, cooked and gossiped. The kids fished, played softball and hiked up to the falls. In the late afternoon, the men would have target practice. They'd set up targets and see who was the best shot with .22 pistol. Early evening, there was a huge bonfire with roasted marshmallows and old-fashioned sing-alongs. By that time, there were usually a few bloody noses, too, as kids got lost, siblings argued and husbands and wives got mad at each other. In other words, it was a good, typical all-American family gathering, with lots of Tyrolean fire.

I'll always remember a gal named Lena Popovich at those picnics. She had a great voice, could sing a cappella, great Italian ariosos—Puccini, Verde. She had a marvelous voice. And she knew it. She was good looking. All the old Tyrolean men had a glint in their eye when they looked at her. And most of their wives were watching.

Winter activities

In the winter, we did a lot of snowshoeing and tobogganing. Ice skating was a big thing in Silverton. It still is. Winters were colder when I was kid, even colder when my mother was a girl. She said that in her time the Animas would freeze solid. On a windy day, with a good headwind, she and her friends would skate down to Elk Park. Then, propelled by the wind, and with their coats spread out like a sail, they'd let the wind blow them all the way back to Silverton. That's seven or eight miles. But every two or three winters, there would be a huge freeze, and they could do that trip easily. Kids raised in the mountains are strong and healthy.

Tombstones and tricks

When we were in the fifth grade, Mrs. Grimes would send us out to the cemetery to make gravestone rubbings. We'd bring paper, rub impressions of decorations and names on the tombstones, like Foxes, Lonnegans, Matties, Andreattas, Dallas, Todeschis. It was interesting, you always seemed to find a stone marker of someone you never knew was there.

Well now, one thing led to another, and pretty soon we found we could make a good game in the cemetery, testing the new kids who came to town. It became one of the initiation rites. You'd wait for a nice moonlight night; take the new kid up to the cemetery during the daylight; and, show them a spot where they had to wait by themselves, armed with a flashlight, which they were supposed to flash at us back down in town. Now, to make sure the kid did what he was supposed to do, one or two of our gang would hide up there close to that tombstone. If the kid didn't go all the way to his appointed hiding place, we'd put on an act, making strange noises, doing "ghost stuff" and scare him silly. The kid would come screaming down the hill. Like I said, nobody had to entertain us.

The trains

The train was (and still is) the lifeblood of Silverton. When I was a boy, there were two lines, the Denver & Rio Grande, which went to Durango, and the Silverton and Northern which went up to Howardsville and Eureka. They ran every day— work trains, freight trains and passenger trains. Some had only one or two passenger cars along with a string of gondolas and box cars. And a caboose.

Every summer my mother would put my sister Jean and I on the train to go down to Durango to visit our Grandmother Swanson. The fare was fifty cents each. Old Miron Henry the conductor, always said, "Mrs. Swanson, I'll take good care of your children. They'll behave for me! "I'll leave them right there at the express delivery office with Oscar Swanson (my uncle)," he'd say. "When he gets off work, he can pick them up and take them up to their grandmother's house."

It took five hours to get to Durango. We had lots of stops along the way for lumber, ore and the Tacoma Power Plant (which is still operating today). When we got to the depot, Henry would say, "Be real good, and you can ride back in the caboose with me, and I'll let you share a bottle of Nehi Orange Soda Pop!" Then, he'd take us back there and let us ride in the cupalo and have our soda.

The Silver Vista Dome Car, June 27, 1947, photographed the first time it arrived at the Silverton Depot. The special car was completely glass-enclosed in the passenger compartment. It was destroyed by fire. Arson was suspected.

Both photos, San Juan County Historical Society

I did the bulk of my riding when I was a kid. In the early 1940s, we'd run down to Durango in the fall to band concerts, and in the spring, the whole band would go down and back on the train. The tracks were in much better condition than the highway, which in those days was the old gravel road along Lime Creek.

For a long time, everything came in—and went out—by train.

The railroads supported the mines, taking supplies up and ore back down to the mills and smelters.

We used to like to watch the trains come to town. The sheep trains were especially exciting. And the coal trains could make us a little money. We kids would go down there, by the tracks, in the summer, with our little red wagons. A lot of coal spilled from the coal cars. We'd gather it up and sell it cheap. Then we'd buy ice cream or candy.

I remember riding the train from Silverton to Eureka, the last year the Sunnyside Mine ran up there. It was about 1937-1938. We rode up on the train with one passenger car. The rest were gondolas and box cars to haul concentrates out to the smelter in Durango. My uncles wanted to go up and see the mine. There was a rumor they

Silverton Northern train tickets
Gerald Swanson collection

were going to shut it down. It was a pleasure to see those three ball mills operating. And it was noisy! With those steel balls pulverizing rock to dust. The train would back in there and pick up the concentrate.

Most of the businesses in Eureka had shut down by the late 1930s. The post office was still open, and Johnny Foreman still had a grocery store up there. There were one or two saloons, a few houses and a mill operation. But the bulk of the people had already moved to Silverton.

There were still a number of people living in Middleton then (the spread of houses between Howardsville and Eureka) and quite a few in Howardsville, which had maybe ten to fifteen houses left. Many of those were later moved to Silverton, and some were moved all the way to Delta, Colorado.

In 1942-43, they started taking up the Silverton Northern rails as scrap for the war effort (World War II). The Denver & Rio Grande cut back on operations, and for twenty years, kept trying to abandon the line. Only through the efforts of a few people in Silverton and Durango were those efforts thwarted.

2003 photograph of the train board as it might have looked in the 1920s and 1930s.
Kathryn Retzler

SILVERTON RAILROAD		
.0	SILVERTON	Ar
5.0	BURRO BRIDGE	
7.5	CHATTANOOGA	
12.5	SUMMIT	
15.0	RED MOUNTAIN	
15.5	VANDERBILT	
16.0	YANKEE GIRL	
17.0	PAYMASTER	
20.0	IRONTON	

SILVERTON NORTHERN		
.0	SILVERTON	Ar
2.0	WALDHEIM	
3.2	COLLINS	
4.7	HOWARDSVILLE	
6.2	HAMLET	
7.4	MINNIE GULCH	
8.5	EUREKA	
12.5	ANIMAS FORKS	

SILVERTON, GLADSTONE & NORTHERLY		
.0	SILVERTON	Ar
3.2	YUKON MILLS	
5.0	PORCUPINE GULC.	
7.0	FISHERS MILL	
7.5	GLADSTONE	

The first tourist train ran to Silverton in 1950. In 1981 the line was purchased by Charles Bradshaw and the name changed to the Durango & Silverton Narrow Gauge Railroad, the tourist operation that it is today. ✳

Above, 2002. The 473 pulls into the Silverton Depot.

© James Burke

Right, 1963 poster for "the Silverton," then a Denver & Rio Grande Western Railroad.

Courtesy the Train Store, Silverton, Colorado

...Take a trip to **YESTERDAY!**
ON THE
Last of the West's
Narrow Gauge Railroad Pioneers
THRU THE
SPECTACULAR CANYON
OF
RIO de Las ANIMAS

The **SILVERTON**

between **DURANGO** AND **SILVERTON COLORADO**

Daily, Saturday, June 8 thru Wednesday, September 4; then tri-weekly—Sunday, Wednesday and Friday - thru September 25 (September 8, 11, 13, 18, 20, 22, 25). 1963

Only **$5.50** ROUND TRIP

Advance reservations: Send check or money order, payable to Denver & Rio Grande Western Railroad, with complete information to Rio Grande Agent, Durango, Colorado, or to H.F. Eno, Passenger Traffic Manager, Box 5482 Terminal Annex, Denver 17, Colorado. Tickets will be mailed to you.

Lv. Durango   9:15 a. m.
Ar. Silverton   12:40 p.m.
Lv. Silverton   2:40 p.m.
Ar. Durango   6:00 p.m.

P.S. For tops in modern travel enjoyment, ride one of these four fine Rio Grande "See-liners":
The Vista-Dome CALIFORNIA ZEPHYR - Daily
Chicago - Omaha - Denver - Salt Lake City - Oakland - San Francisco via CB&Q-D&RGW-WP

The PROSPECTOR - Overnight, every night
Denver - Salt Lake City

The Vista-Dome COLORADO EAGLE - Daily
St. Louis - Kansas City - Pueblo - Colorado Springs - Denver via MP-D&RGW

The Vista-Dome ROYAL GORGE - Daily
Denver - Colorado Springs - Pueblo -
Glenwood Springs - Grand Junction - Salt Lake City
Thru car Denver Zephyr service between
Chicago and Colorado Springs via CB&Q

DENVER & RIO GRANDE WESTERN RAILROAD
Passenger Traffic Manager - Rio Grande Building, Denver, Colorado

✂ Three ✂

Chickens & Chores

Chickens got me in big trouble with my mother when I was about seven. My mother used to keep chickens for my Uncle Herman at the Dalla Boarding House. Those chickens used to get out, and it was my job to catch them and put them back. Well, we also used to play around the old county jail. And there was this cook, Ed Fay, who cooked one meal a day for the old pensioners over there. We'd hang around, and he'd say, "When I get done feeding all them old people, I'll give you some of this gawdamm pie." "Gawdamm" was one of his best expressions. Well, I got back to the house one day and had to round up the chickens, and I was on the porch, shooing the chickens out of there, saying, "Get out of there you gawdamm chickens!" when my mother heard me.

She grabbed my collar and jammed a half bar of Life Boy Soap into my mouth. Life Boy soap was strong. I never used that "g" word around my mother again, even when I was grown and married. If we used that Lifeboy treatment today, maybe kids would be better behaved.

Everybody had chickens back then. We kids used to steal them and take them up by the Animas River and cook them. We'd sneak up to somebody's backyard and grab the chicken. If you just grabbed it, it would squawk like heck. But Fatso Gallegos had a better way to do it.

Uncle Herman Dalla
Gerald Swanson collection

He'd strike a match and stick it under the chicken's beak. The sulfur was just like ether. It'd knock the chicken out and he'd fall down. Then Fatso would stuff it in a gunny sack. One of us would steal a fry pan, Howard Hill would steal a pound of lard from his mom, and Jimmy Jorsted always brought a salt shaker. We had some "big people" ideas, I guess. We'd take that chicken, strip and skin it, cook it up. We thought we were Cochise, or somebody, cooking out there. Most of the time we had so much flame, it was just a lump of charred flesh.

My friend Arthur Candelaria said one time, "We can steal my mother's chicken." We stole two and cooked 'em. His mother asked who did it and he confessed. She called all our mothers and told them we were stealing her chickens. All three of us got punished and promised never to steal chickens again.

The next day we started stealing rabbits. They were easier to skin, but they didn't taste as good.

Coal bins and bathtubs

When we moved to this building (the present Dallavalle Inn) in 1938, the windows were busted, there was no insulation or central heating, and it had great,

big old high ceilings—very drafty. It was like a barn. The windows rattled. Frost formed on the walls, and you could lie in bed and scrape it off with your finger nails.

In the winter you slept in your long johns, wool hat and mittens. You dressed like an Eskimo most of the winter.

There was a coal burner in the front room, where we had the grocery store, one in the little living room parlor in the back and the coal burner kitchen range.

Firing a coal stove was an art. Lots of young people came up here in those days who never knew how to fire them. The stoves were always going out. It required lots of cleaning to get the soot out and ashes off the grate so the fire would get a

Historical items, Ouray County Historical Museum

James Burke

good draft, pull the smoke up and keep burning. That was my job everyday, to clean (rake) out the ashes under the stove, haul them out and dump them in the alley. I also had to split three baskets of wood for kindling and bust up the coal into fist-sized chunks.

Coal was the cheapest way to heat, though. We had one freight dealer, Micky Logan. He had four great big Belgian horses and hauled coal up and down the alleys with a wagon. Logan would dump the coal in the

"My mother had an old Maytag washing machine. I had to cut up the Fels-Naptha soap for washing clothes."

Historical photos, Ouray County Museum, James Burke

backyard, and it was my job to keep the coal buckets full. We burned eight to ten coal buckets a day, in a twenty-four hour period. We'd take anywhere from twelve to fourteen tons of coal in the winter. My mother said it was the best feeling when she had enough coal to get through the whole winter instead of buying one ton at a time. One of her favorite expressions was, "I'll be so happy when I can afford to buy enough coal to last through the winter!"

We all had chores, all the kids in Silverton. We had to shovel snow, do dishes, split wood, bust up coal. On Mondays I helped my mother get out the wash tubs to do the washing. We had an old Maytag washing machine, which was a really no more than a one-speed agitator with a wringer apparatus on the top, and two galvanized tubs, one for hot water, one for rinse water. One of my jobs was to cut up the Fels-Naptha or P&G (Proctor and Gamble) bar soap. You'd shave it off with a knife, into the water, so it would melt. A lot of people made homemade soap with lard. Later, when I was in the meat business, I'd save the lard and give it to the Spanish ladies to make soap. They'd give me some of the prettiest soap imaginable—colored and scented.

For the sheets, and white things, we used "bluing." In the summer, when the weather was nice, you could hang out the sheets (although you'd have to haul them in before the train came, or they'd get sooty). In the winter, though, you had to string them all over the house, on wires, ropes, the back of furniture or the pipes from the coal stove.

Water was more plentiful then. Of course, we didn't have electric dishwashers, clothes washers or

Barber chair and pole.

restaurant systems. We strained out impurities in the water by tying gauze over the faucets. In the spring, especially, a lot of junk came through the faucets—twigs, leaves and dirt from the snowmelt. Over on Greene Street, we usually left the fire hydrant running all the time. In case of fire, you could just dip out of the runoff.

I remember sailing little boats down that stream when I was a boy. It ran along the west side of the street, from the Wyman building all the way down "main" (Greene) street. The old miners would sit on the stoops in front of the buildings, whittling. We called them "spit and whittle boys." They would whittle for a while, then spit. You had to be careful when you were sailing your boats along that little stream!

Dentist's chair doubled as barber chair. Ouray County Museum

James Burke

When the miners came to town, one of the first things a lot of them wanted was a haircut, shave and bath. All the barbershops had bath houses. I remember Curtis the Barber and George Bolen. George had three bathtubs at his place. It cost a buck for the haircut, six bits ($.75) for a bath or a shave.

We weren't as clean then as we are today. You'd use your towel over and over until it was so ripe you could stand it up in a corner. For most families, especially those with kids, Saturday night was bath night. You'd get out the old galvanized tub, heat water on the coal stove then pour it into the tub. One thing about those old galvanized tubs. When you touched the side of them, in the winter anyway, they were cold. But when your bottom hit the bottom it was mighty warm. When my aunt Lena moved to a new house, she had a bathtub. My sister and I used to take baths in it—at the same time. They'd put us in back to back, and my mother would say, "Now Gerald, don't you be looking at your sister!"

Of course, you didn't linger in there. The water would cool off pretty fast, and we all had to take a turn at it. And we didn't have central heating. Or insulation. You hurried to clean up, get out and get dressed again.

Outhouses. People ask about that. Most times, the outhouse was not attached to the house. In winter, you had to shovel a path out to it. For inside, we had "thundermugs." We didn't have toilet paper; we used old catalogs. The sewage disposal was the Animas River, even after the downtown was plumbed. We didn't have a sewage treatment plant until the 1950s. Once we moved into the building on Blair Street, we did have an inside toilet.

Manure and mayhem

We didn't keep many horses around in those days, most of them shipped out on the train in the fall. But a lot of people kept cows for the milk and cheese and cream. At one time there were four dairies in town: Berigenson's, Tomasi's, Perino's and Augustine's. (The last dairy in town was run by Norman Wells, it's up where Greenfield has his church now.) After they'd milk them in the morning, they used to drive the cows up 10th Street, across "main" (Greene) street and up Anvil Mountain. In the evening, they'd bring them back down again to milk them. They used cow dogs, who could separate the cows from the different dairies by the sound of their bells.

James Burke

In the winter, they'd have to keep the cows in town, in the barn or in fenced-off areas near the barns. The dairyman would have to shovel his way out to the cows. Talk about a good, sloppy mess with all that snow and shit. Sometimes they'd run planks out to the river and have hired hands haul all that manure out and dump it in the river. Or they'd stack it in piles where people could come get it in the spring.

Cow manure makes good fertilizer. Cows have four stomachs so they digest all their food. It's not like horses. Use that manure and you get a garden full of weeds, cause that's mostly what's in it.

I milked cows with Bernard and Henry Bogolino for Augustine's (Joseph Augustine.) It was a pretty messy job in the winter, cold and miserable. I had the great experience of snow, ice, manure and milk. You'd get up early when it was cold and dark, shovel shit, wash down the barn, haul hot water from the house kitchen out to the barn to wash the cows' udders, then milk them. I got paid two quarts of milk and ten cents a cow per day. Never did more than four cows a day. After school I'd help Mrs. Augustine wash and sterilize (with hot, soapy water) the bottles for the milk.

When the milk was delivered to the house in the winter, it was put on the stoop. At five below, if you left it there for a few minutes it would freeze. The cream would come to the top and pop the wooden cap off. It'd be like a cream popsicle. Milk in those days was so rich it was about half cream. You'd take off a little for coffee and save some for homemade ice cream with vanilla. We used old crank ice cream makers.

I didn't last long at milking for old man Augustine. He was a Tyrolean (Austrian/Italian), and he liked to drink. He got mean when he drank. He'd come into the barn and get mad when a cow kicked him. I remember one time he doubled up his fist and hit this cow, knocked it down. The cows didn't like him and shied away from him when they saw him coming. One winter, he got real drunk and fell down. The cows jumped on him, stomping him around in all that shit and muck. Old man Augustine just got up again and took another swing at those cows.

Ladies on the Line

I ran errands for several of them. For the most part, they weren't welcome up on Greene Street, so I'd go pick up groceries for them, or a bottle from Crippled Mary at her liquor store, which was a little store on the the west side of 12th and Greene Street. Or maybe get something from the dry goods stores. They'd usually give us kids a generous tip. When I ran errands for Big Billie and Blondie, for instance, they'd usually give me a quarter. That was a lot of money—a shot of whiskey cost twenty-five cents.

Now those girls weren't bad girls. Often as not their occupation came about by circumstances. They were just hungry. Life in a mining town for women was harsh. There weren't a lot of job opportunities for women in those days. Women weren't allowed to wait tables or clerk in stores. Only men could have those jobs. So women were relegated to menial scullery work unless they got married. And even scullery work was scarce. So, a lot of women took the

Examination certificates for "ladies on the line."
Gerald Swanson collection

Outside Matties' Welcome Saloon on Blair Street (where Natalia's is today). Back row: Innocente Girardi, Anibule Girardi, two Girardi boys, Ricardo Roccabruna. Front row: Joe Matties, Girardi girl (stripes), "Crippled Mary" Matties (who owned liquor store on "main" street), Mrs. Girardi, Ottilia Matties and Jack Matties (brother of Ottilia's husband who lived in the Dalla Boarding House when I was a boy. (He is referred to as "Caco" in stories in this book.)

Courtesy Lucy and Bill Walko, Natalia's 1912 Family Restaurant

easy way out and worked the line. Many of them lived in a "crib," a little one-room shack with just a wash basin and a bed. (The name comes from a baby crib, meaning there was a minimal amount of living space.) Others, who had been living with a man who beat them, moved out, became a hooker for a while, then moved in with another man. It was a tough life. A lot of those women got pretty despondent. There were a lot of suicides. On the other hand, some of those girls got respectable and married local men and had a pretty good life after that.

The thing is, though, out of vice, if you want to call it that, grew a lot of good things. Those girls were the greatest groups of donors. They helped raise money to build churches, buy necessities for needy families and take care of a miner's widow and children. My mother used to tell me stories about the gals from the line. They were like a form of Red Cross workers during the flu epidemic. They would volunteer their time, give comfort to the sick—maybe a mother, father, all the kids were sick—wash clothes, wipe sweat off brows and offer comfort when people were in agony. They'd be there for some poor old prospector who was down on his luck, sick, maybe dying from cirrhosis of the liver or rocks in the box (lung's box, silicate in lungs, like glass, or "miners con" is a disease that eats up the lungs, leaving the victim to die from lack of air, like black lung from coal mining). They would take up collections and raise money for burial and tombstones. As far as I was concerned, these people were a very fine breed of people. If they had legalized prostitution, we would have had less disease, loose behavior, unwanted pregnancy, crime and dope.

There were still some hookers left right up until I was in high school, maybe about eight or so when I was a boy. The Mikado ran into the 1940s. "Box Car Kelly" (Olie Kelly) worked there for several years along with Pearl Thompson (better known as "21 Pearl") and "Big Billie," who eventually bought it. "Jew" Fanny shut down just after that. I was about twelve or thirteen when she left town. I remember a gal named "Blondie" (they also called her "Babe" and "Blondie Peggy"). She never had a house, just floated between the Avon, Fanny White's place and the Hood Rooming House.

"Nigger" Lola, (Lola Daggett) was one of the last to leave. Her original house, south of where Natalia's is now, was attached to Matties' Welcome Saloon. After it burned down, she worked out of a place that is now the Emporium at Old Town Square. Her nephew used to come over with us to Giacomelli's. He always had money for candy, and he was always willing to share.

Today's Shady Lady Saloon on Blair Street is the same color as the old "Green House" that served as a four-girl crib from 1897 to the 1940s. (2003 photo)
Kathryn Retzler

"Nigger" Lola Daggett and one of her girls. (Building on the right is Matties', now Natalia's.)
Courtesy San Juan County Historical Society

"Tar Baby," a mulatto (light black person), married a local man who at one time was sheriff in Silverton. Mrs. Pacotti had a house across from where the Silverton Hostel is now (at present, a real estate office). For a while, she had been married to a guy named Pacotti, but after he was gone, she needed the money. She was pretty old for a hooker.

Big Billie wound up in Telluride, running a beer hall over there. When she was in Silverton, she had two gals in there with her at the Mikado. The building has since been torn down. It was next door to where the Lookout is today, just north of

Gilheany Gambling Hall and Murphey's Cafe, site of the present High Noon Hamburgers.

Fanny White's place was part of the building where the Shady Lady is now. Next door to it, the taller building always had a couple gals working there. One of them later on married a guy named Blake and became very respectable. Fanny White was friendly with my mother and used to shop at Swanson's Market. When she was leaving town, my mother asked, "Miss White, why are you quitting business?"

"Well, Mary," she replied, "It's not that I don't like Silverton anymore. It's just getting hard for a decent woman to make a living here anymore, what with all those other women giving it away free in bars!"

Fanny White moved to Denver with her husband, Mr. White, and became a respectable citizen.

Jobs for kids

There weren't many during the depression. But there were a few things kids could do to earn money. Stacking lumber for the hardware store earned fifty cents an hour. So did working as a day janitor after school for a grocery market or business. Running errands for the hookers and mowing lawns was worth a quarter. Of course you had to furnish your own mower. Picking a bushel basket full of dandelion buds to make dandelion wine got you twenty cents. It takes a long time to fill a bushel basket with those buds. And I mean a long time! (Mrs. Slobonick used to make the best dandelion wine. She'd mix the buds with water, sugar and yeast and they'd ferment down to a nice, amber-colored wine.) Manual pin setting earned you a nickel a line. Collecting, cleaning and turning in wine bottles got you ten cents a dozen. And selling scrap back to the junkman got you a penny a pound.

Now, to put that all in perspective, a Sunday afternoon movie cost ten cents. A shot of whiskey, which us kids couldn't get, was a quarter. A loaf of bread or a bottle of milk was ten cents. And a nickel bought you a cube of butter.

My mother started the grocery store, Swanson's Market, in 1939-1940. Bread was shipped in from Durango. We sold it for ten cents. A bottle of milk cost us seven cents, and we sold the milk for a dime.

Delivery boy

Starting when I was in fifth or sixth grade, every Saturday I'd deliver groceries for my mother. Before I could drive, I'd use a wagon, or in the winter, my sled. Later

Grocery store items like those carried in Swanson's Market.

Edith Eggett collection,
Ye Olde Livery, Silverton, Colo.

I used my mother's old truck, and it became a lot easier. But before that, I'd spend most of Saturday walking around Silverton.

The old gals I delivered to were a nice bunch: Katie Fox and Mrs. Maxwell, both on Reese between 9th and 10th; Mrs. Eilleson, on the corner of 9th and Reese; Mrs. Brown on Reese between 8th and 9th; and, Mrs. Nelson clear up on Reese and 15th. There were two on Blair Street, Mrs. Foster, north of us, between 13th and 14th, and Mrs. Pacotti, between 10th and 11th. The reason it usually took all day, most of them had other errands or chores for me to do. Mrs. Fox was short, so she'd have me dust her lamps and cookstove. Mrs. Maxwell had me bring in coal from her backdoor to the coal shed: it was always full of snow. Mrs. Brown wanted her mail picked up and delivered. Mrs. Pacotti, nine out of ten times, wanted two quarts of port wine. She'd give me the money and a note and send me up to Crippled Mary's Liquor Store.

Those women didn't have a heck of a lot. There was no social security or welfare. The county would give them a ton of coal a month and maybe $20 for groceries. It was hard living. And there was no sitting around watching television. Most people didn't even have radio. If they did, all they could get was KOA out of Denver and KSL out of Salt Lake City—depending on the weather. For radio reception, they'd have some kind of outside antenna. You'd turn on the radio and it would go squeakin' and squawkin' and then come back on.

Where the money went

One of the places we liked to spend our earnings, besides the movies, was at Art Lorenzon's Post Office Drug Store or Joe Dresback's Blue Cross Drug Store. Both of them had comic books. And both of them had big signs that said, "Please do not read the comic books." Comic books cost a nickel apiece. They had "Flash Gordon

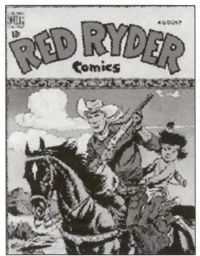

Red Ryder
Courtesy Fred Harmon III

of the 21st Century," "Tarzan of the Apes," "Barney Google" (a comic character), "Maggie and Jigs" and "Kats and Jammer" (about two little mischievous German boys who were always in trouble). I especially liked "Popeye & Bluto." Bluto was always the villain. And "Wimpy" who was always making wimpy burgers. We also read "Captain Marvel," "Captain Mercury," "Superman," "Green Hornet," "Gene Autry," "Roy Rogers," "Red Ryder," and "Little Beaver."

When you got a chance to go down to Durango, you could find some things that weren't available in Silverton. What I liked best about shopping in Durango was that it had a Woolworth's store. For me, that store was a world of dreams. They also had a Ben Franklin. For a dollar, you could buy three balsa wood planes that would fly, or three kites, or a good rubber ball was twenty-five cents. I also got my first BB gun from Woolworth's. You shot one BB at a time, had to cock it between shots, so as not to waste BBs.

You'd spend all your money at Woolworth's, then come home to tell your buddies what you saw. Then you'd start saving up for the next trip down there, working at extra jobs around town.

I'll always remember going downtown to the old Silverton Hardware, between 12th and 11th on the west side of "main" street. It was between what is now the Brown Bear and Romero's Restaurant. It was a big, two-story hardware store and sold everything from paint to barbed wire, to dynamite, to roller skates. It always had the best supply of Flexible Flyer sleds with big, high runners. I still have a six-foot Flexible Flyer that my kids and grandkids are still using. It's over forty years old, maybe older. Going into that hardware store, I always marveled at the newest things—like toasters, electric mixers, things we didn't have in our house, the latest wood-burning stoves, different kinds of nails, saws and lumber. I always liked to watch the old plumbers thread galvanized pipe and put fittings on it. That was an education in itself, going to the hardware store. They used to buy all the empty wine bottles my sis and I could find. They'd clean and sell them again, filled with coal oil or turpentine.

Silverton also had the Carl D. Curtis Hardware store up on "main" (where the Orange Crate is now). He outlasted the Silverton Hardware by several years. I worked for him one summer, hauling lumber from flatbed cars on the railroad up to there, and stacking it. You had to hoist six and seven inch beams and stack lumber you could hardly lift. It didn't pay much, though.

We also had wallpaper stores. One of the better wallpaper stores was run by a lady named Mrs. Closter (south of where Ye Olde Livery is today). Mrs. Closter had the last wallpaper store in Silverton. She carried all kinds of sizes, shapes, patterns of wallpaper from the 1920s through the 1940s. She was a withered-down, stooped, scary old lady who always had two or three black cats in her store. She reminded us kids of a Halloween witch.

Elton McJunkin had the livery stable (in the foreground). Just to the right is the building where Mrs. Closter had her wallpaper store.

Kathryn Retzler

When I was in grade school, the teachers would have us make May baskets. We'd cut out paper flowers, paint and decorate them, then deliver the baskets to different people in town.

Somehow, I'd always get Mrs. Closter. She had a little bell that rang on the door when you opened it. I'd see those big old cats staring at me. The wallpaper in there had been there for decades.

Mrs. Closter was taller than me by four or five inches. "Young man what do you want?" she'd ask.

"Well Mrs. Closter, I brought you a May basket," I'd say.

She wore these half gloves—it was so cold in there—and the tips of her fingers were black from firing her coal stove. She'd look down at the basket, and with a tear in her eye, she'd say, "You just wait a minute young man."

Then, she'd dig in her apron pocket, get out a little snap purse, wiggle her finger around in there and come up with a dime. A dime was a lot of money in those days.

Everything was harder then. People didn't have the money or resources they have today. We had to economize, make do with what we had. You never threw away paper, you saved it to light the coal stove. You saved wood for kindling, and when it was wet, used coal oil to ignite it.

I was in the fifth grade when the war started (with the bombing of Pearl Harbor.) We all learned how to roll bandages "for the war effort" and to knit little squares (for afghans for the soldiers). We also looked for tin foil—gum wrappers and cigarettes were good sources. We spent the summer gathering scrap iron, too, and sold it to Elton McJunkin. He paid two cents a pound. Sometimes we'd sell it to him, then steal it back and sell it to him again.

He had the livery stable up where Edith Eggett is now (Ye Olde Livery) and used to store horses up there on the second floor. He had an elevator to haul them upstairs and back down again. And he had all the junk downstairs. It was quite a place. Smelled, too. *

✂ Four ✂

Town Characters

There were a lot of characters around town when I was growing up. We've got a few now, too. Those were hard times, back in the '30s. People were hungry. There weren't any social services to provide for widows and old prospectors. People just had to make do.

Hans Tanstad

There was this one old boy who liked to whittle—Hans Tanstad. Now, Hans had a wooden leg he had made himself, being a carpenter. He'd lost the real one working at the Gold King Mine near Gladstone. A log had rolled down the hill and crushed his leg, so they had to amputate it. Anyway, Hans would sit on the stoop of the Orella Building (now the Crewel Elephant), which was a liquor store at that time. He'd sit out there whittling, and we'd go by with a new kid in town in tow and introduce him to Hans.

We'd talk a while, then we'd say, "Would you like to see what Hans can do?"

The kid would nod, and old Hans would grab his knife and jab it right into his leg. That kid would about have a heart attack! Then Hans would pull up his pant leg and show the kid his wooden leg.

We lived across river in the old boardinghouse then. (It wasn't a boardinghouse anymore, just our home. With twenty rooms and a big, scary cellar filled with old wine casks, it was a great place to play.) We'd stop to visit with Mr. Tanstad when we were on our way to town to get the mail. He'd reach in his pocket for his purse, which had three little snap compartments, and come up with a nickel for each of us. We'd stop at Fiore Giacomelli and Rosie Tinor's Confectionery just up on the corner, where we could get two or three pieces of candy for a penny. We'd shop and talk for a while with old lady Giacomelli. She'd always give us a good deal on candy. It was always a good trip to see Hans once a week.

Hans had a horse named Frank. Now old Hans, he liked his drink. He lived over on the flats. "Chinese Gardens" they called it. Hans would come to town on his horse, and if he got too drunk to get on the horse, and nobody would help him, Frank would get him home somehow, even if he had to walk him. Hans didn't fare so well with automobiles. He died in a car wreck up on Ironton Flats.

B.O. Plenty

His real name was Dave King, but we tagged him B.O. from the character in the Dick Tracey cartoons. The guy was real dirty and smelled pretty rank. He had long, straggly hair (like Howard Hughes). All the kids were afraid of him.

B.O. and his old sway-backed horse lived in the dump ground down by the Animas River. He had made himself a hovel out of old tin. They both lived inside! The horse pulled an old iron-wheeled cart. They'd go around picking up everybody's ashes, charge fifty cents a load, then take them to the dump. Sometimes he'd go meet the train and sit there, with his sway-backed horse and iron-wheeled wagon. The tourists would take his picture and he'd make enough money to by a quart of Muscatel wine.

Poor old B.O was always the butt of jokes. One day they found old B.O. Plenty behind Giacomelli's and thought he was dead. They took him up to the hospital. Dr. Holt (more on Doc Holt, later in this chapter) had to cut B.O.'s clothes off. He was so dirty they were literally glued to him. They put him in the bathtub with two gallons of coal oil, soaked him to soften his skin, scraped the dirt off and cut his hair. After he was clean and sobered up with new clothes, B.O. walked downtown.

No one even knew him.

Well, it didn't take him long to get back into his old ways. He rounded up his horse and hitched it to the wagon. Before long he was grungy, not as grungy as before, but pretty grungy. He got sick and destitute again, so the welfare director, Fenrick Sutherland, gave my mother an order that they would send his welfare check to her. He couldn't hang on to the money—spent it all on that Muscatel. This way, with my mother in charge of his checks, he'd at least have money to eat on. He'd come in and buy a little tobacco, lunch meat, bread and a jar of jelly. He loved gingersnap cookies and hoop cheese (longhorn cheese; it came in a round wheel, weighed about 7 to 8 pounds). Mother saved the leftover money. After a couple of years, she'd saved a total sum of $98.

The meaner kids or dogs chased him. When he got very sick and passed away, my mother used the money she'd saved of his to buy him a tombstone, which is up in the south end of the cemetery.

The Bertramsville Flemings

Wilfred "Fat" Fleming was a county commissioner and the mill superintendent at Sunnyside Mill in Eureka. He was a real politician, a smooth operator. Every time he'd come to town with his wife Helen, he'd come into my mother's grocery store and ask Mary to give him a sample of her Gorgonzola blue cheese. Then he'd ask for "maybe a couple of slices of Italian Genoa salami, too."

"My God," said my mother, Mary, "maybe I should slice up some bread for you too, since you have lunch here nearly every day!"

Some years later, I used to deliver groceries for Mrs. Fleming. They lived in Bertramsville, just north of town. It was a pretty area with lots of trees. The Flemings had a television set, and Mrs. Fleming could never figure out how to tune it. So when I'd make a delivery, I'd have to "fix" it for her so she could see her programs.

"Caco" Matties

Jack "Caco" Matties was a short, Austrian/Italian who always smoked Peerless tobacco in a curved pipe with a big brown bowl. It was the strongest, stinkiest tobacco you ever smelled in your life. He'd let it harden in the bowl, scrape it off with a pocket knife, put it in his mouth and chew it!

Caco (Italian slang for "Jack") lived at the Dalla Boarding House with us for a while. He was always kind to my sister and I. When he went to town to do his shopping, he'd always bring us a little sack of candy and leave it on the stoop for us at the boardinghouse.

My mother used to wash his clothes, and in return, Caco would cut wood for her. One time, he came home with a great big sack of what looked like colored candy, but it was actually colored stones for a fishbowl. So, we took the "candy" back to old Caco and told him what it was. He went over to the French Bakery, where he had bought it, and came back with a big sack of regular candy.

My sister and I used to like to have lunch with him. He'd fry potatoes and onions in a big heavy skillet, with

Jack "Caco" Matties always wore an Italian Alpine hat with a light grey feather in it.

Photo, Lucy and Bill Walko

a lot of lard, pepper and salt, and have it with his coffee, which was mostly sugar and milk. He probably put two or three tablespoons of sugar in a cup of coffee. We thought it was a wonderful lunch.

Primo Segafredo

Primo was another fellow who liked his tobacco charcoaled. He worked up at the Sunnyside. When he came off a "man trip" (a one-man hoist or elevator) after his shift, he wanted his tobacco. All the men smoked pipes in those days, but they couldn't smoke underground. So they left their pipes in the "doghouse." (This was the little room where the miners kept their mine lamps, personal items, lunch buckets and so on. It was a place to rest your "dogs," your feet.) Anyway, when he came off shift, the first pipe he came to, Primo would scrape out the bowl. Then, he'd keep scraping bowls until he had enough tobacco for a chew.

Art Lorenzon

Mr. Lorenzon had cash registers on every counter of his Post Office Drug Store, so named because at one time he had a store up the street (where Whistle Stop is now) that had a post office in the back. When he moved up the street to the building that is Hold Your Horses now, he called it the same name.

The red brick building on the corner of 13th and Blair, now Hold Your Horses, was once home to Art Lorenzon's Post Office Drug Store. (2002 photo.)

Kathryn Retzler

He had registers by the soda fountain, the school supplies, the office supplies, in back where he sold pharmacy and patent drugs and prescriptions, over where he sold cameras and odds and ends and novelties. Every day he would count out a certain amount of money and put it in each register. At the end of night, he'd take the receipts, count the money and make sure the right amount was in each register. Then he'd take every one of those damn little register drawers out and put them in his big safe.

He had an old Wurlitzer Juke Box in there—it played old 78s. Six songs for a quarter. And a great comics rack. All the kids tried to steal comic books from Art Lorenzon, or they'd sneak back there and read them. When he caught them, Lorenzon would throw the kids out.

Art Lorenzon liked to eat at the Best Cafe, and he loved to put coffee on his breakfast cereal. And he put ketchup on everything he ate. Mashed potatoes, meat, everything. When he got done, he was a mess. He spilled half of it on his shirt most of the time.

Jess Carey

Jess was a chef, a bartender and a really great baker. He worked the restaurants, mining camps and boardinghouses all around the mining districts, but mostly in Ouray and Silverton. He'd also been a mule skinner.

Cakes were his specialty. That man could really decorate cakes. He made beautiful strawberry shortcakes with real whipped cream, and he would put red roses on top. When he made lemon meringue pie, the meringue stood up at least four inches and it never did fall. When he was decorating cakes and making roses, he'd always stick the cake decoration tool in his mouth to keep it moist, but I didn't care for that.

Old Jess never smoked or drank that I knew of, but he did have a vicious temper. The last place he cooked here was the Club Cafe and Bar (now Fetch's) owned by Bill and Svea Mowat.

One year for Thanksgiving he baked four big turkeys. Well, that Thanksgiving, for some unknown reason, people got to drinking and they ordered hamburgers instead of turkey. Jess got real mad and told Bill Mowat, "I ain't going to do no more cooking in the damn cafe. All they want is hamburgers!"

Jess Carey with actresses Virginia Mayo and Ruth Roman, who co-starred with Raymond Burr in the western movie, "Maverick Queen," made on Blair Street in the 1950s. The photo was taken in the Bellvue Saloon, built in 1899 by Phil Sartore (now Zhivago's). It was called "Red Ash Saloon" for the movie.

Gerald Swanson Collection

Jack Johnson, World Heavyweight Boxer, with chef/bartender Jess Carey in the Western Hotel, Ouray, early 1900s
Ouray County Historical Society

Jess threw his apron at Bill, dumped the turkeys in the garbage and walked out.

In the 1950s Jess Carey moved into a building on Blair Street (where Zhivago's or the "Deli" owned by Marvin and Diana Paioff is now). It was formerly a saloon built by Phil Sartore, then owned by the Troglia family. Jess opened a saloon museum, the Free State Saloon—so named by the movie company who used it for a movie that Virginia Mayo, Ruth Roman and Raymond Burr were in. (More on movies, see Chapter 6, "Hollywood Comes to Silverton.")

In his museum, he always demonstrated how to stack dishes and set the table. Jess could carry eight boardinghouse plates at one time!

Every so often, Jess would get mad at my mother, Mary, "I'm not trading with you anymore, Mary Swanson," he'd say. "I'm going over and trade with Julia Maffey at the French Bakery."

Then he'd get mad at Julia, and she'd call up my mother and say "Jess is coming back."

Jess passed away 1968 at the age of seventy-nine.

Ben Bagozzi

Ben was a good drinker. He used to get in fights on Blair Street with his hard-drinkin' buddies, Cornito (Italian Don Juan) and Coustantie (also a slang name). They'd all get drunk in one of the bars, spill out into the street, stand on either side of the street and throw rocks at each other. The cops would come and calm them down.

Ben lived in a little shack down on 11th and Mineral. One day he went into the Carl D. Curtis Hardware store, and they told him, "For a bachelor, you need to buy this Presto Pressure Cooker. You put everything in there: your meat, your potatoes, then put in some water, seal it, put it on top of the stove and cook it a couple of hours. You have to put this top on here so it don't explode."

Old Ben came up to the market and bought some beef shanks from me, and some potatoes and onions and carrots. This was when I was helping my mother run the store in the 1950s. Ben says, "I'ma gonna makea me a big pot-a soup. And I'ma gonna putta in this pressure cooker and cooka it down. I don't got so much teeth no more," he says. "It's hard to chew."

So, Ben goes home, puts everything in the pot on top of the old coal range, and he gets the range going real good. But he forgot to the put the escape valve on top of the cooker.

Ben was sitting by his table when the damn thing exploded. It blew him off his chair and right through the front door. The explosion disintegrated the top of the pressure cooker, blew the top off his stove, blew stew all over the front room of his bachelor's quarters. A neighbor came over and helped him clean up.

Old Ben, he took that pot back up to Carl D. Curtis and said he wanted his money back because the pot exploded on him. "No more," he told me when he came in the store the next time. "No more I'ma gonna cooka the stuff in that kinda pot. I'ma usa the regular pot."

At one time, Ben had the highest number of lawsuits going in San Juan County. He was always jumping somebody else's mining claim. Then they'd sue him. Ben would actually go to court with a lot of these people. I remember a famous mining attorney we had here, William Way. He was very tall, very skinny and looked like Ichabod Crane. When I was a young man, Mr. Way was talking about Ben Bagozzi one time. He said he liked mining law, but didn't like dealing with guys like Ben, who always had a lawsuit going. "I finally had to tell him I wouldn't defend him anymore. I was sick and tired of his damn shenanigans!"

So, Ben Bagozzi went to Ouray and hired an attorney there who had a reputation of being a little bit shady himself. And Ben went back to jumping claims.

Louis Dalla

Uncle Louis (pronounced Looey) was a great storyteller and boxer, and he had a great singing voice. When he was young, he worked on and off at odd jobs. He sold newspapers and coal and ran errands for the ladies on the line. His first job, at age eleven, was driving horses and mules from Bayfield to Silverton for the Mattivi brothers.

Louis was a tough little fellow. That's him on the right next to his brother Fury. Notice the pugilistic expression. He was always ready for a fight.

Gerald Swanson collection

Later he was a lineman for Western Colorado Power. He also worked at the Shenandoah Dives Mine and the Mayflower Mill. He was a road worker—worked for the county for a while as a heavy equipment operator and worked for the Colorado State Highway Department. Louis Dalla served twenty years as a county commissioner, and he had a particular interest in the welfare of old people. He was the first commissioner to push a law to buy at least one ton of coal for old-age pensioners. (About a $2 value.)

He was also a scrapper. The dances he went to often ended up in a scrap. He also boxed for money, including when he helped to raise money for Silverton's first motorized fire truck, a 1927 Chevy.

Uncle Louis had a mind of his own. He lived over at the boardinghouse, which my mother was running, and didn't like some of her rules, even though she favored him over the other kids.

One time, at age eleven or twelve, he ran away from home. Mary said, "I think he got on the train and rode to Durango." She called the sheriff, and he wired down to Durango. The police chief there met the train. Sure as shoot, there was Louis Dalla, packing a bag. He had a big, long-barreled pistol with him, too, with one bullet in it. For protection, I guess. Louis was always worried somebody was going to "get him." (He wasn't scared of much, but he was scared of Billy Goat Gruff and the people he imagined were hiding under the bridge at Cement Creek.)

Louis told the police he was going down to Mancos to the farm. (We still had the family farm down there.) So they put him on the next train to Mancos. My mother let him stay one week, but then he had to come back, 'cause he was "playing hooky from school."

But at the end of that week, he still hadn't come home. My mother wired the marshall in Mancos to send him home. Uncle Louis told the marshall he was having such a good time riding horses and fishing he forgot about coming home.

The marshall put him on the next train.

Louis didn't like my mother's cooking much. He never wanted to eat his supper. So, she'd bribe him with money for candy if he'd eat it. Even before he'd finished his bowl of soup or stew, Louis would jump up and head out to buy candy.

Another time, back in the early twenties, Louis and some of the older boys rigged up a block and tackle and hoisted a big mule up on one of the roofs going into one of the entrances of the big red schoolhouse. And they also hoisted up part of a small outdoor outhouse right up on top of the school. It was over on Reese Street, our big school house over there, the red one. Not on the high building, but they had these little roofs on the back edges. But, that was still about fifteen feet off the ground. I guess it created quite a

Silverton's first motorized fire truck was a 1927 Chevrolet. Louis Dalla helped earn the money to buy it by boxing. (Photo from July 4th Parade, 1976.)
Gerald Swanson collection

commotion. It took a bunch of adults all day long to try to calm the old mule down to get him off the roof. To this day they never could figure out how a bunch of young kids ever got that mule up there.

His brothers always said Louis was my mother's favorite. Uncle Herman told me later that anytime Louis went someplace, like on a basketball trip, Mary would give him two dollars, and he didn't have to bring home the change. "She gave me only one dollar," Herman said. "And she always asked me for the change."

Herman Dalla

Even though Uncle Herman and Louis may have had their differences growing up, they wound up the best of friends. Herman boarded with Louis and his wife Lena. They both worked on highways around the county, and they both worked for the state highway department. Uncle Louis was Chief of Maintenance for the San Juan District of the state highway department.

1938. Louis and Herman Dalla.
Gerald Swanson collection

1940. On the road to Ouray. Herman Dalla on the bumper of his new 1930 Chrysler

Angelo Dalla photo
Gerald Swanson collection

All the boys, including my Uncle Herman, loved my Aunt Lena. Herman never knew his father; he was born after his father died. And he was only six when his mother died. Herman was born April 15, 1912. He always said, "On the day I was born, the Titanic sunk and taxes were due. You don't think I was born to trouble?"

Uncle Herman built the Prospector Hotel and ran it for many years. He worked out a deal with his sister, Aunt Rena, who at that time was running the American Legion Bar. She'd go down and run the "mangle" (roller iron) in the morning for Uncle Herman's sheets at the motel, then go up the street around noon and open the Legion Bar. She always brought her lunch in a sack.

If Uncle Herman needed something during the day, he'd have her lock up and come down and run the motel. She would put a sign on the door, "Be Right Back."

Herman sold the motel to some people named Fuchs. (Yeah, it looks bad, but sounds like "fewks"). Then, he helped Rena out by running the bar at night. Rena would fill the beer coolers during the day if Herman forgot to do it at night. She was a tough little old lady.

Guys would get off swing shift (or the early shift) and come down to the bar for a beer. All the mine buses stopped in front of the American Legion. Men would come in with their pie cans and muddy boots. In winter, the mud in the Legion Bar got pretty thick. The men would have snow and ice on their boots. It would melt and drip

1980. Bernard Bogolino, ??, Steve Smith, Uncle Herman Dalla in front of the American Legion Bar.

Gerald Swanson collection

1990. Herman Dalla ran the American Legion Bar for many years.
Gerald Swanson collection

onto the floor, which had to be mopped several times during the day. Many of the miners would sit at the round table up front. It was the closest table when you came in the door. And there was a nice warm radiator there. So guys could warm their butt and have a cold beer.

Rena Dalla Antonelli

My Aunt Rena (Mary's sister) married Fidenzio (Phil) Antonelli when she was fourteen. They bought the Pastime Bar and Cafe (now the Brown Bear) around 1945, right after the war ended. Uncle Phil passed away in 1950, but Aunt Rena ran the place until Phil Jr. came home from the service (after World War II) to help her. It was one of the best watering holes in Silverton. All the miners came in there. It was a local bar owned by a local family.

Rena sold the Pastime to Dean Joseph in the late 1950s, then she went on to become the full-time manager of the American Legion Post 14 Bar. When she took over, we moved the bar up front. Before that, it had been in the back, where the dancing area is now. Up front was a library and game room for the Miner's Union (AFL-CIO).

Before Aunt Rena managed it, members tended bar on a volunteer basis. The Legion was open Wednesday for Rotary Club, Friday for American Legion Bingo and Saturday for the Lion's Club. Then, we decided we needed more space for American Legion, so we moved the bar up to front and took the bookcases, mining journals, books and so on to the basement.

1955. Mary Swanson and her sister Rena Antonelli with son Phil Antonelli.
Gerald Swanson collection

We had a Legion meeting one night and talked about running the bar full time. Aunt Rena said, "I can run it for you guys. Give me a small percentage. It gives me something to do."

She had a Coors Beer sign in the window. When Rena flipped that on, she was open for business. She also went down there everyday before noon and opened the bar. And she stayed until midnight.

Supposedly, this was a private bar. People weren't allowed in there unless they were Legion members or guests. The Legion had a private license. But Aunt Rena would never lock the door. So, we were challenged many times, and we got closed down many times because of it. Aunt Rena was a tough old lady.

Every bar she ever worked in, she called 'The Joint." Each morning, at 7:30 a.m. on her way to "the joint," Aunt Rena would stop by the market (Swanson's Market) to visit with her sister, my mother, Mary. At first, it would be very amiable. Then they would get in an argument over their customers.

"Well, Rena," Mary would say, "have you seen so and so? He hasn't been in here in over two months to pay his bill."

Rena would say, "He's good customer at the bar. Pays a little bit at a time. He's such a good guy."

Mother would want to garnish his wages. Rena would get mad, stomp out, "By God, I'm not coming down and see you anymore, Mary," she'd say. A couple days later, she'd be back. "Where's your mother?" she'd ask when she came in. Then she and Mary would have coffee in the kitchen, and all would be fine for a couple of days.

Then along came another day and another fight.

After I was married and lived with my wife Stela and kids up on "main" street, my mother would come for breakfast. My wife would cook and my Aunt Rena and Uncle Herman would show up. My mother would warn Herman not to eat all the pancakes or bacon. Herman would go off in a huff. Rena would take his side and stomp out to open the bar. Then everything would calm down again and be fine.

But we still had some of the best fights up there on "main" street.

During the summer, sometimes my mother and Aunt Rena would go riding on Sundays in her 1956 Scout. They were dangerous. My mother would putt along, taking her time. They went up to Animas Forks even when she was seventy-five years old. They'd wander all over those back roads. One time I asked Aunt Rena, "Don't you get nervous up there? Aren't you afraid you'll get stuck?"

"No," said Aunt Rena. "I don't pay any attention. We just visit. Your mother drives."

Frank Salfisberg

He was the postmaster when I was kid. We used to call him "Deacon." He and his wife, Helen, were both heavyset, but boy could they run. During the Sheepman's Days mining events, when there'd be a footrace, he and Helen could outrun all us kids.

Salfisberg was a pillar of the community, a big shot in the Democratic Party, and the vice president of Silverton Fish and Game Club. He also served as town marshall, night marshall, day marshall and water commissioner.

Frank Salfisberg
Gerald Swanson collection

One time, he and a couple of other guys, including Frank Hitti, who was president of the club, started rounding up stray sheep left behind in the fall roundups. They put them in Augustine's corral, thinking they'd make a nice meal later, some nice roasted mutton. Somebody mentioned to the cops there were eight or ten sheep in the dairy barn, and the cops came looking. It was quite a scandal when they found out who the culprits were.

Frank was postmaster, his wife was assistant postmaster, and they had one other clerk, Eda Tomasi. She worked for the Silverton Post Office for over twenty years, until she moved to Durango.

Italian hen party

There was a group of old ladies, Italian friends of my mother's, who we used to visit every Saturday. Our first stop was at the house of Lucy Maffey. (Her real name was Letizia. She was Julia Maffey's mother, grandmother to my best friend, Lynn Murray.) She lived upstairs on "main" street, over the French Bakery. Mother would stop to pay her respects. Lucy would always give my sister and I an Italian macaroon cookie. While the ladies visited, my sister and I sat on a little bench in the kitchen. All the Italian houses had them.

The rest of the ladies lived on Blair Street. We would stop to see Mrs. Andreatta. Everybody called her Lena, but her real name was Maria Angelina Zanoni Andreatta. Lena wasn't much for sweets. She always gave my sister and I either an orange or an apple or some grapes. From there we'd go up to Mrs. Matties' house. She always gave us a glass of homemade root beer. Our last stop was Mrs. Othello Orella. She was always good for some hard candy. These Saturday

1940s. Lucy (Letizia Caradini) Maffey, mother of Mary's friend Julia Maffey, Lynn Murray, her grandson (and my close friend), with Lena (Maria Angelina Zanoni Andreatta) on the roof of the French Bakery.
Gerald Swanson collection

visits were great, because we got treats we didn't get at home. It was something to look forward to. All the women were very fine cooks, very generous people.

Once a week or so they'd get together at Mrs. Maffey's house and have a real Italian hen party. Most times Margaret Troglia would join them. Usually, I'd be upstairs, playing with Lynn Murray. They'd be in the little parlor up there, drinking grappa (Italian whiskey) or Italian wine and smoking — the only time any of them smoked palley malleys (Pall Mall cigarettes). You can just imagine, those little old ladies, all smiling and yelling, laughing and arguing, and talking real fast in Italian. They'd also eat boiled chicken legs. (Nobody wasted anything those days.) They'd break off the ends and chew them like you would chew nachos or popcorn, and those chicken legs would crackle when you ate them. It was a real Italian hen party, a little drinking, a little puffing and a lot of chatter and laughing.

Dobbie Burnell

Dobbie was another drinker. His parents owned a two-story building on 11th and Greene, a famous old home on the east side of "main," across from the American Legion Bar. Dobbie used to work for street crews for the city and county. He'd go into the bar and drink his lunch. He'd drink his dinner, too, and after dinner, he'd drink his desert — more Schlitz beer.

Dobbie was a good old boy, but his biggest fault was Barley Corn. (That's what they make beer out of.) He could drink a sixteen ounce bottle of beer in two swallows.

Dobbie Burnell's family home, across from the Miner's Tavern. (2002 photo.)

James Burke

Johnny Jenkins was another regular who made the rounds with Dobbie and his friends.

Gerald Swanson

I watched him do it many times in Aunt Rena's Pastime Bar. (Now the Brown Bear.) After he finished his beer, Dobbie would light a Chesterfield cigarette, smoke about half, then order another beer.

He'd do the same thing all over again, easily consuming eight to ten sixteen ounce beers during his lunch period. (All beer came in sixteen ounce bottles those days.) After his shift ended at 5:00 p.m., Dobbie would be right back at the Pastime Bar with buddies like Harry Turner, Fatty Turner, Johnny Jenkins and Phil Antonelli Sr. Their next stop would be the Chili Parlor (on "main" street, where the Enamel Shop is now, next to the Funnel Cake shop). The Chili Parlor was run by Nora Bolen, and it was next door to the barbershop she ran with her husband, George.

Anyway, Dobbie and his friends would go there, or maybe stay at the Best Cafe and have roast beef. One way or another, they would usually wind up at the Pastime and stay until it closed up around midnight. Dobbie had a great capacity for beer, but he died a relatively young man, in his fifties.

Dobbie Burnell

Gerald Swanson

Dr. Frank Holt

He was the resident physician at the Miner's Union Hospital in the '50s. He was a real genius, a super mathematician, historian and brain surgeon. Doc Holt had lots of degrees; he was really well educated. He had also been kicked out of the hospital where he worked in Denver.

Dr. Holt, you see, liked his I.W. Harper. Silverton was just the right place for him. There were plenty of bars in town.

Doc Holt would park himself on a barstool around two o'clock (when he was supposed to be at the hospital) and have a Harper, washed down with a side of beer. He also smoked the longest cigarettes in town. Twelve hours later, someone would take him to the door and point him toward the hospital and home.

That's where he lived—the hospital. It wasn't exactly the cleanest place in town. He had ten or fifteen cats roaming around the hospital and newspapers put down in all the rooms for the cats. He didn't clean them up. It got pretty rank in there.

He finally moved out, over to Blair Street. Once he was gone, the county had to hire two guys to go up and shovel it out and fumigate. They worked nearly a year inside there cleaning it up.

Doc Holt settled into an old crib on Blair Street, right next door to the old Bent Elbow, owned by the Andreattas at the time. They had just bought the building. Doc Holt practiced medicine out of his one-room shack and made a few house calls.

He kept clean for a while. Then one bitter, cold winter night, he went on a real good toot. When he came home and couldn't get a fire going, he threw what he thought was coal oil on the glowing coals in his stove. It turned out to be white gas.

That cabin exploded. The front blew out and blew him out with it, pitching him into a snowbank. The fire blazed up and set the old Bent on fire. It was so cold out, only one of the hydrants worked—I was on the fire department at the time—and we had a hell of a time putting the blaze out. The Bent Elbow was destroyed, but the Andreattas made a deal with the people who owned the Monte Carlo and remodeled it, and that bulding is the Bent Elbow today.

Miner's Union Hospital, home of Silverton's "drinking doctors." (2002 photo.)
Kathryn Retzler

Doc Spencer

Silverton had some doctors that, like their patients, became great consumers of "demon rum." When Doc Holt left the county hospital, and after it had been cleaned up, the county hired Doc Spencer. He was a drinker, too.

Doc Spencer was a goofy guy. I remember one time, a while back when I was president of the Lion's Club, he went with Phil McClosky and me to the state Lions Club Convention in Denver. When we started out, Doc Spencer said, "You drive the car, Gerald, I'm going to drink all the way."

At Grand Junction he bought a whole new set of Goodyear, double eagle, white-wall tires for his car. They were the most expensive tires out those days. And more booze. We stopped in Rifle so he could see a friend. On the way, Dr. Spencer rolled down the window, took out his twenty-two pistol, and started shooting at signs as I was driving down the road!

Phil McClosky said, "Hey doc, you can't do that."

Old Doc Spencer turned around, pointed his pistol at Phil, and replied, "Hey Phil, you want one? I'll put one right between your eyes."

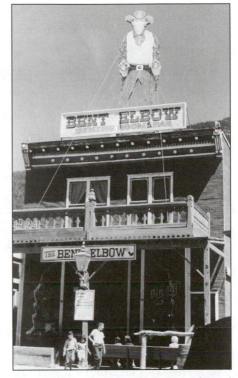

The old Bent Elbow on Blair Street burned down when Doc Holt, who was living in a crib next door, poured white gas on glowing coals in his stove.

Gerald Swanson collection

He was also a little crazy. I remember one time—this was in the 1950s—Doc Spencer had been on a drunk for about two weeks. He came by the Columbine Tavern and Texaco Station, owned by Uncle Angelo Dalla and his partner Louis (Louie) Visintine.

Dr. Spencer told Louie to put gas in his car. Louie didn't understand him—he was hard of hearing. Well, Doc Spencer got mad, pulled out a rifle and threatened to shoot Louie, who ran through the station, jumped out a window and escaped.

A couple of years before, you see, a robber had come in the Columbine when Louie was tending bar there and demanded money. Louie thought he was asking for food, and told him, "n-n-n-no." (Louie stuttered, too.) The robber asked again, and when again he was refused, shot Louie in the belly. Louie had no stomach for getting shot again, so when Doc Spencer threatened him, he ran!

Meantime, the doc jumped in his car and headed for Silverton. Uncle Angelo called the sheriff, alerted him the doctor was headed to town, drunk, with a big, big rifle.

Doc Spencer roared into town and up to the hospital. He ran in the front door with his rifle, climbed up to a top-story window and started firing. Shots went all over town. People were running, ducking and hiding.

George Bingel heard the commotion. He had a 30.06 with a scope on it at home, and he was a very good shot. He went into the hospital and checked the situation over, then drove down the alley across the street and went into a two-story building (which is still there today). He opened a window and waited until Doc Spencer poked his head out with his rifle. George shot that rifle right out of his hand! Meantime, the sheriff went up the back stairs, found the doctor and tackled him. They sent Doc Spencer to Pueblo to the insane asylum.

Corky Scheer

No reminiscences about the characters in this town would be complete without talking about Corky Scheer. He was one of my favorite characters over the years. Corky was born here into a pioneer family. He was a hardrock miner, a hellacious drinker and a damn clever fellow. I watched his shenanigans as I grew up. Corky was the kind of guy who would take any challenge. He'd be in a bar drinking, which he did a lot of, and somebody might challenge him to eat a light bulb.

Corky Scheer
Courtesy Zeke Zanoni & John Marshall, *Mining the Hardrock.*

We'll, he'd bust that light bulb up, and he'd eat it.

Once, word got around he was having a fling over at the Club Cafe and Bar (Fetch's building today). Corky had a running bet going he could eat ten large night crawlers as long as he had a lot of beer to wash them down with. He had no trouble winning the bet.

Corky had a heart of gold and would help anybody. When he was sober, he'd give you the shoes off his feet. But, when he was three sheets to the wind, he was the most obnoxious little snot that ever lived. He agitated every cop we ever had in Silverton.

Corky was short and wiry. What he lacked for in height and strength, he made up for with a loud mouth.

He was the principle lead man in the town's water fights that we had over on Blair Street in those days. There were no paved streets in town then. The pressure from those fire hoses was so great, the water would pick up rocks. People didn't want to break the windows on "main" street. I remember little Corky in front, holding the hose with Bob Caine (we called him Cousin Jack, as in Union Jack, after the British flag from England) right behind him. Corky was hit full-breasted with a stream of water from the hose. The force knocked Corky down and rolled him down the street, through all the rocks and muck.

Corky Scheer, from Silverton Then and Now *by Allan G. Bird.*

Allan G. Bird

Corky made some pretty good money mining at one time. He and Ole Olson, Frank Hitti, Barney Blackmore and a couple of others had a lease on the Pride of the West Mine. They hit a high-grade vein up there and all came out smelling like a rose. That was fifty-five or sixty years ago, and they all made about fifty to sixty thousand apiece. That was good money in those days.

The first thing Corky did when that mine hit was come back to town and buy a brand new Dodge four-door Sedan from L.W. Purcell's Circle Route Garage. Then he bought some really good suits. And after that, he didn't drink swill anymore, only the best whiskey.

Corky's luck and money ran out about the same time. By then, I was the San Juan County Veterans Service officer. My job was to help vets—Corky was a veteran who served a year and a half, then got a

The Benson Hotel, on the corner of 12th & Greene, today is home to Citizens State Bank. (2002 photo.)

Kathryn Retzler

deferment to come back and work in the mines—with filing claims for pension, hospitalization, travel money, etcetera. Corky was still tough, although in his wanning years he had no insurance.

When he came back, for some unknown reason, Corky had lost all of his hair. He was completely bald (and didn't have any body hair, either). I filed a claim for disability for him. We went to Grand Junction, then they sent him to the V.A. Hospital in Salt Lake City, trying to determine what he'd developed while in service that made him go hairless. The ruling came back, he had contracted a viral infection, and the only thing they could do, the only government benefit available to him was a wig, which he refused, of course.

Corky was drinking pretty heavily then, but the government did not recognize alcoholism as a disease back then. The V.A. refused to take him every time I sent him to Grand Junction. They would sober him up, get him some new glasses and dentures and keep him until spring when he was in good shape. When they let him go, he'd come back to Silverton and go on a tear again, until he was destitute.

One time I drove him up there in a snowstorm, then drove all the way back, getting home at midnight. When I went to work the next morning, at 7:30 a.m., there was Corky, right in front of the Benson Hotel. He'd hitched a ride back. When I called the V.A., they said, "We don't want Mr. Scheer again. It's the third time he's gone AWOL on us."

Corky had a hard time defeating the booze, although he did eventually make it. In the meantime, he probably spent more time in the Silverton jail than anyone in town. Every so often, they'd haul him in, sober him up, feed him and assign him tasks for the city, like shoveling snow or coal or chopping kindling.

As soon as he got out, he would go on a toot again. I remember one time, Corky was living in the alley behind the Benson in an abandoned Chevy. He had been drunk for months. Art Weibe, the night marshall, knocked on my door at home.

"I need some help," Art said. "I got old "Tracks-Or-No-Tracks" Martin (Corky's friend), and he tells me Corky is behind the Benson, and he's dying."

So we go up there. It's cold as hell. I opened the back door of the vehicle and the stench was so strong, I almost fell down. Art dragged Corky out into the snow. We rolled him over and put him in the patrol car. I met them at City Hall, where we had the jail in those days. We stripped Corky down, put him in the shower—only cold water. That sure woke him up! Art handed him an old sponge and heavy-duty soap. We helped scrub him. Corky was shakin' from the cold and the DT's. When he was clean, we wrapped him in boardinghouse blankets, set him on a bunk in the jail cell and dressed him in old clothes.

Eventually, Corky sobered up and settled down. He got married (for the last time; he'd tried it a couple of times before with no success). He and his wife bought a motel at Carlsbad Caverns, New Mexico, where they stayed for eight to ten years. Then they moved to Delta, Colorado, where his wife was from originally.

Sloppy Jack, Billy McGuire and Moon Mullins

When I was about ten, Sloppy Jack died. He was an old miner, a pensioner, who always walked around town looking kind of sloppy. He died, penniless, in the Miner's Union Hospital, so the county buried him. I was an altar boy at the time.

Billy McGuire, who had the mortuary at the time, brought him up to the Catholic Church in a hearse. His helper was a guy by the name of Moon Mullins, who was a worker for the Western Power Company but helped Billy out now and then. It was the custom for the priest and the altar boys to go to the church doors and stand there, up ahead, to help lead the coffin in. The church had four rises or steps. Billy was a short, wiry guy. He backed the old 1920 Buick hearse (called the "Black Mariah") up and started to pull the casket out. It was a flimsy, wooden coffin, with pink and green covering. Billy told Moon to get up ahead of it.

I was standing on one side of the priest. Howard Hill was on the other side. We were both holding candles. Billy bumped against the steps and jiggled the coffin. Moon dropped his end, the end with Sloppy Jack's head in it.

Billy McGuire
Gerald Swanson collection

The casket flew open and Sloppy Jack rolled out onto the sidewalk. It scared me half to death!

Billy put his end down, ran around, grabbed Sloppy Jack by the hair and jammed him back in the box. He gestured to us boys to help him cram him back in there. Then he slammed the lid on.

My mother, Celia Todeschi and Aunt Rena Antonelli were all there at the funeral. The three of them came up to help, and when they saw what he did, got mad and started reaming him out. All this happened in front of the church before the funeral even started.

George Sitter

Old George was a cook around town. He cooked in restaurants and boarding-houses and owned several restaurants. His wife was Jinks Sitter. I remember when George was the chef at the American Cafe in the Grand Hotel (today, the Grand Imperial). I had hired on as a young man to help in the kitchen, cleaning pots and pans along with my cousin Clyde Todeschi.

In those days, the back bar served as a dish storage area in the restaurant. It had been moved over from the saloon to where the lobby is now, which is where the restaurant was. Old George, he was a fine baker and a decent chef—he loved to cook big boardinghouse meals: lots of meat, potatoes and veggies boiled to death, but he was cantankerous as hell. He was pretty clear about what he liked and didn't like, and one thing he didn't like was cooking hamburgers. Well, he was back in the kitchen, grumbling about something, when the door flew open and Jinks burst in. "One hamburger," she says, "lots of ketchup and onion. No mustard."

George plopped his meat clever down on the meat block and screamed, "What SOB wants a damn hamburger this time of day!" He stomped toward the door. Jinks didn't say another word. George goes out to the dining room, Jinks on his heels. She points at the priest. George glares at him, goes back in the kitchen and makes the hamburger. All the time he's cookin' it, George is saying, "I hope he chokes on it."

George was also our judge back then. He approached judging like he did cooking and dispensed quick justice. George Sitter would say, "Well GD, Johnny, you wouldn't be here unless you were guilty."

The first time George hit the gavel, you were fined 19-6 bits ($19.75). The second offense was $39.50. The third offense was a flat $100 and two weeks in jail, but you could get time off for good behavior and work. The city had work programs like scrubbing down the city hall and raking snow or rocks into piles.

There wasn't much crime then, maybe an occasional knifing or bar fight. A few guys got shot. And, of course, we had our share of domestic fights. If one happened in a bar, the barkeep usually let them fight it out, unless it got too serious. Both parties would get their licks in, then go home and make up.

Fred Patterson

Fred was a member of a pioneer family that settled in here. He worked in law enforcement all around San Juan County. He was also a personal friend of Herman Dalla.

They both liked to fish. Uncle Herman told me about a time they were down on Cascade Creek fly-fishing. Fred was behind Uncle Herman as they were going down the creek. They came around the bend, casting quietly into the pool, then looked up and saw a little old black bear on the other side of creek. He was fishing too, swatting at the water, looking for trout. Fred kept his pistol on the bear, just in case, but he was enthralled watching him.

Then Fred got a trout, and he got so excited he slipped off the rock and dropped his reel into the creek. The bear took off in one direction, Fred in another. He rounded up Uncle Herman and they both walked down the creek, looking for the reel. They found it up on a bank, its side in the sand and the remains of a trout sitting there. The black bear had eaten Fred's trout.

Fred drove a Terraplane car. One time, when he was sheriff, he had a brand new convertible and he drove it over to Mrs. Mattivi's house to answer a complaint. (She lived across Blair Street, where the Hitchin' Post is now.) In those days, people kept goats and chickens, and every so often, they would get out of the yards and wander around town. The goats liked to climb everything and chew on everything.

Somebody had complained that Mrs. Mattivi's goats had torn up their garden and eaten the radishes and lettuce. While Fred was in there talking to Mrs. Mattivi about it, her goats worked their way down the alley and out to the street. They climbed up the back of Fred's brand new car and on top of the canvas top.

They fell through. Neighborhood kids started yellin'. Fred came out runnin'. He saw the top shattered and the goats sitting in his front seat! He got so damn mad he served Mrs. Mattivi with a warrant, hauled her into court and fined her $15.

You know what? Mrs. Mattivi's goats never did get out on Blair Street again after that.

Fred was a well-respected member of the Masonic Lodge.

Fred Patterson, San Juan County Sheriff (1930s) and John Troglia (who married my cousin Celia Todeschi), circa 1940. The men were coming up from Durango in Patterson's Terraplane automobile.

Gerald Swanson collection

He died here of a heart attack during World War II. They had the funeral over at the Masonic Lodge on 13th and Reese Street. More than 200 Masons, members of the Eastern Star and law enforcement people came to the funeral. ✳

Five ✒

Basketball & Buddies

For the seventh grade, I had several teachers. The men had been called to war, so it was mostly women. Boys had to take home economics (sewing, not cooking) so they could learn how to sew on buttons and knit afghans.

Eighth grade was a time of transition, the worst age of disobedience, I think. We were always coming up with ways to get into trouble. One of the boys in school, Lynn Hadden, was a real rabble rouser. He led a revolt demanding school be let out when President Roosevelt died. (Lynn never did like school.) The superintendent went to his house and demanded his mother teach him at home for the rest of the week. As for the rest of us, we were given time out to sing "God Bless America." Then we were back in class.

Above: My 7th grade class, 1941-42. Front row: Henry Bogolino, Jimmy Drobnick, Clee Robinson, Carl Peterson, Robert Montoya, Clyde Todeschi. Middle row: Carleen Larson, Helen Kennedy, Gladys Antonelli, Dorothy Knoll, Mary Moretti, Roberta Montoya, Jackie McClary, Helen Loback. Back row: George Romero, Jimmy David, Layton Melburg, Superintendent Duke Dunbar, Lynn Murray, Richard Maes, Gerald Swanson.

Gerald Swanson collection.

Hanging out

We weren't allowed to drive, but we did. My group had cars, an old '39 Chrysler, Model A, a Dodge. Old clunkers. Down at our Youth Center, we had a Rock-olla jukebox that would play old 78 records. "Platters" they called them. That was one of our best hangouts when we were getting up into junior high and high school. We used to also hang out at the soda fountains, like at Art Lorenzon's, where we could get flavored cokes—cherry, vanilla and lemon. Those were all the rage in the '30s and '40s.

There were a lot of dances, even during the war. They had them a lot of places, like the Miner's Union and the Fireman's Hall. Kids under eighteen were not allowed in dances unless they were with their parents. There were dances for kids, too, at the school and at the Youth Center. The boys would sit on one side of the room, the girls on the other. During the war, 1940-45, there was no television and radio was very poor up here. So we used to get records—Glenn Miller, Jimmy and Tommy Dorsey, Eddie Duchin, Frankie Carl, the "Big Bands." And piano—Les Brown, Band of Renown, Harry James. It was an era of great music. We did a swing at Teen Town and had a lot of fun. Everybody tried it.

Above: My 10th grade class, 1945-46. Front row, teacher Miss Greer, Roberta Montoya, Mary Moretti, Helen Loback, Dorothy Knoll, Carleen Larson. Back row: Lynn Murray, Richard Maes, Carl Peterson, Billy McGuire, Gerald Swanson, Clee Robinson, Clyde Todeschi, Jimmy Drobnick, Layton Melburg. Not shown: Billy Gentry and Buster Everett.

Gerald Swanson collection

What I always wanted to own, and couldn't afford, was a flat porkpie hat and a zoot suit. This was a fad toward the end of World War II. The pants ballooned out at the knees, pegged at the ankles. The coat had huge shoulders and was tapered at the waist. You wore a big key chain with it. I used to think that was so cool.

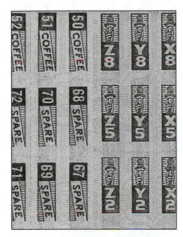

Above: ration stamps. Below right: ration stamp booklet, front and back.

Rationing and the war effort

We were still in a war economy in 1943 and 1944, and things were still rationed. We had ration stamps—red for meat, blue for groceries, yellow for gasoline and tires. (All the tires were retreads, and the inner tubes had so many patches they looked like one big solid patch.) The number of stamps you got was determined by the size of your family—so many for sugar, beef, bread.

Things you couldn't buy (except on the black market) were new tires, candy bars and name brand cigarettes. The newspaper office issued all of the stamps. You could also pick them up at the Post Office.

Ration stamps were like money. At Swanson's Market, we'd keep track of the stamps and deposit them in the bank. We'd use them as credits to buy for the grocery store. There was a lot of bartering going on. If a person had two good inner tubes, for example, and needed twenty gallons of gas, he could trade for it. If you had a carton of Camel or Lucky Strike cigarettes, you could really wheel and deal. A full carton of Camels would trade for ten pounds of sugar or flour.

Tea and coffee were also rationed. You could buy coffee, but it was blended with chicory. Tea was easier to get until the war, then there were no shipments of tea from the Orient. We could get oranges around Christmas, but no other time. We did have apples, though. They were kept all winter long in a barrel in the basement. The ones that kept best were the little sour ones like you used for making pies. Most of the

housewives knew how to can fruit and vegetables. So in the fall, everybody would buy bushel baskets of corn, beans, tomatoes, peaches and apricots. We'd can for nearly a month. My sister and I helped mother wash all the jars and sterilize them. We'd use rings and later we got new caps. When it became difficult to get caps, we'd buy old ball lids with rubber gaskets. Lids were on the black market, too. The war effected the entire country. Ingenuity was the name of the game.

People faced with that kind of adversity today, might not survive. They wouldn't have the experience to figure out how to manage.

Everybody got on the patriotic bandwagon, including cigarette companies. You saw advertising that said, "Lucky Strike has gone to war." Their cigarettes used to come in green packaging, but the green foil was used to make camouflage stuff. So, the new packaging, if you could find Lucky Strikes at all, was white, although it had the same familiar red circle logo.

Lard and honey (for cooking and baking) were available, but you couldn't get sugar or oil. Butter was rationed so tight that a family could have only a half pound per week. Oleo margarine was used as a substitute. It was basically a vegetable oil in the consistency of lard and margarine that came in a white block. One of my jobs was to drop yellow food coloring in it and stir it up. It was just like stirring lard—old fashioned margarine was plenty thick. People never heard of it before World War II.

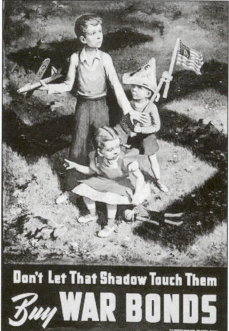

Soap was another hard-to-find commodity. You couldn't buy Oxydol,

Rinso, Lux or Dreft. And although you'd buy Fels-Naptha in the bar, you couldn't buy Lifebuoy. Laundry soap (for dishes and clothes) came in big paper drums. Another job my sister and I had was to separate the powdered soap into little paper sacks and tie them. It was so strong it would burn your hands when you sacked it.

"Lucky Strike Green Has Gone To War." (The green dye used for the packaging of the Lucky Strike packs went to the war effort.)

Since you couldn't get sugar, honey was used as a substitute. My mother made a deal with a farmer down in the Animas Valley. She could get twenty 5-gallon cans of honey down there. But the honey man didn't tell her the honey was full of dead bees. So my mother came up with a plan to clean it. We put the honey in a bucket on the old coal stove and heated it until it was warm and runny. Then, we'd pour it into Kerr canning jars, straining it through gauze and fine strainers to get rid of the bees. Sometimes it would take all night to go through one 5-gallon can.

You could buy soda in a bottle, but in those days, soda was a rare treat. People didn't go around drinking four or five cans of soda a day. And there was no such thing as diet soda. My mother used to make root beer soda from root beer extract and honey.

Everybody helped in the war effort. Girls in Home Economics classes were taught to sew, crochet and knit, so they could make stockings and afghans for the soldiers. They rolled bandages, too. The boys also learned to knit. We spent half an hour every day knitting little colored squares which the teachers then hooked together into afghans.

For our shop classes, the government brought in machine lathes to machine metal parts for defense, like screws. Once a week we wrote letters to soldiers overseas. We were like pen pals.

The women went to work in the factories, and the girls all wanted to be like Rosie the Riveter. The boys all thought of Colin P. Kelly, one of the first airmen of World War II, as their hero. We had pictures of him going down in flames over Germany, piloting a B-17, "Flying Fortress." One of the popular songs in those days was "Praise the Lord and Pass the Ammunition."

Meat—we had plenty

My mother had an "in" with the Vanderpool Packing Plant in Delta, Colorado. She would take them all the meat stamps she could get, but George Vanderpool always gave her a little bit extra. Once in a while, he'd give her a whole smoked ham. Every week my mother and I would drive her 1939 chevy sedan to Delta, and she'd always take the back seat out of the car so we could stack the beef in the back. We'd buy half a beef, and a hind quarter of beef and a half dozen pork loins. Then, we'd load that old Chevy up and come chugging back over the mountain. Sometimes we didn't know if we'd be able to get over the pass and back home again. Winter nights, I got pretty good at putting chains on the tires. My mother would put that car in low and we'd crawl over that pass. She'd always time it so we got out of here early, and out of Delta by ten, so we'd be coming up mid-day from Ouray. They didn't plow the roads in those days at night. It was all gravel road then—better in winter for traction; but in the spring, there'd be so much mud, you'd slip and slide all over the place. One thing I liked about old Vanderpool, he'd keep an eye on us. "Mary," he'd say, "let's check your tires—see if you're safe to get home." And if he found a tire that didn't look so good, he'd look around out back and round up one of those old, used, vulcanized tires.

When we got home with the meat, one of my uncles, usually Angelo, would pack and hang the meat in our cooler. The next morning, Charlie Person, who was our meat cutter, would be here between 5:30 and 6:00 a.m. He'd take off his galoshes and unwind the wraps on his legs. Mother would make him hot coffee. He'd drink it, then go out and start cutting meat. Old Charlie was still doing it when he was eighty years old. When Charlie got too old, Frank (Ike) Bausman (who spent twenty-five years as janitor for the county courthouse), came down and cut meat for my mother, and by that time I could help a little bit, too.

The old 1927 Chevy fire truck from those days is still used in parades today. That's me on the running board in a recent July 4th parade.

Gerald Swanson collection

Junior firefighters

A lot of the men had been drafted, including many of our local politicians. Frank Brown, the fire chief, came to the school and recruited a bunch of us boys. You had to be sixteen to serve as a volunteer fireman. Some of the old fellows were still around to critique and train us. The senior boys served as the "chiefs," and the rest of us, we were kind of "auxiliaries."

We had an old 1927 Chevrolet fire engine, a small pumper. There were two fire sirens in town, one at the south end by the Mobile Gas Station and one up at City Hall. When the fire siren went off, we'd drop whatever we were doing and run like hell to get to the fire. It would blow three times real loud, stop, then blow again. That meant everybody should dash up to City Hall and load up the old 1927 Chevy.

Everybody helped. There weren't any parades to speak of in those days, so a fire was a big event. The whole town would turn out.

One of the biggest problems was frozen hydrants. We had bad winters during the early '40s, and a lot of the hydrants would freeze up. Nothing would come out when you turned it on, so you'd have to hunt around to find a hydrant that would put out some water, sometimes stretching the hose all the way out.

The firemen's meetings were a big deal. They were held up at City Hall once a month. There was a critique, and maybe a little practice, but mostly it was a social occasion, with a keg of beer and a Dutch lunch served on an old miner's "pie plate" (great big hot dogs, a batch of beans, sour and dill pickles) and treats for the kids. George Sitter would bring homemade doughnuts—baked cake doughnuts. Before the war, the firemen used to box up there. After the main match, the kids used to square off. There'd be a lot of bloody noses and a few tears, then the food would be on, and everybody would be friends again. The firemen were fed first, then the kids got to eat. They always had pop for the kids.

Basketball

I started playing basketball when I was a freshman. We didn't have a band then, and a lot of teachers (male) were in the war, so there weren't a lot of extracurricular activities. We had a great basketball team during 1946-49. Our team even went to state. All of my teammates have passed away or moved away.

Basketball was the only thing we really had. There were no school buses in those days. The way we got to games, adults would take us—four or five of us, all jammed together in each car. We traveled that way all over the place. The roads and the passes were not so good in those days. There wasn't any Coal Bank Pass; it was Lime Creek Pass, a gravel road over Spud Mountain to Durango.

So when we went out to play games around the area, we stayed overnight. A lot of times it was a four-day trip to play basketball around the region. The schools were good to us, put us up, and fed us.

When we played in Ouray, we'd stay all night at the Beaumont Hotel. God, that was a beautiful hotel! The next day we'd drive to Telluride. We always stayed at the old Sheridan Hotel. It was a dying, elegant hotel then, built during the heyday of mining industries. We all remembered this gal named Big Billie who had been on the line in Silverton. She "got respectable" when she moved to Telluride during World War II and opened a 3.2 beer parlor and dance hall. We'd go visit her place after the ball game. The pretense was to visit with Billy. She'd want to know what was going on in Silverton. The coach would come down and find us and threaten expulsion—no more basketball if we hung out there.

Then we'd go down to Dolores. They had a great big gymnasium. But there was one problem with that gym—they used to store dry beans in it. So it was always dry and dusty, really dirty. You'd dribble down the floor and the bean dust would fly up. It looked like a cloud of smoke in there! The Dolores people were really good people. Ruby Vighil was a cheerleader. So was Glynis Litten. There were a bunch of neat young gals down there we were all half in love with.

1946. Gerald Swanson
Gerald Swanson collection

First five district all-stars, 1947-48. Litton (Bayfield), Robinson (Silverton), Alley (Pagosa), Springer (Dolores), Murray (Silverton). Silverton had two men on the All Stars!

Gerald Swanson collection

One time, we were staying at the Del Rio Hotel. It had just been remodeled. The guys got a little rowdy. This kid, Walter Gallegos, picked up a fire extinguisher and sprayed foam all over the new rugs. Then Clyde Todeschi and Kenny Smith got in on it, and there was a foam fight. The school ended up paying $400 to the hotel. Clyde and Kenny took the rap so the first team, who had started it, could still play in the game.

The following weekend, the Ute team came to Silverton. These were Ignacio Utes from the Agency School, and they talked in Ute. They were also the fastest runners we ever had to play against. And we were really fast, because we came from such a high altitude. One year we were really hot, running neck to neck with the Utes. I was dribbling down the side line and this big Ute stuck his leg out and tripped me. I fell, cut my head and was bleeding. My teammate Richie Maes said, "I'm going to get that big Indian!" He dribbled down the court by the sidelines, then pretended to slip and hit the guy with his knee—and got him the jaw. It started a near-riot. The Ute Police came in to calm everybody down, to take us apart. We finished the game. And we won.

Next we went to Dove Creek. It was the worst place we played. The gym was so small, they had the backboard painted against the wall. If you didn't come to a complete halt, you slammed into the wall when you went up for a basket.

The second worst place was Bayfield. The gym was in the second story of a great big old hall over the Conoco gas station. The rafters were exposed in most places. You had to shoot a straight ball or it would go up in the rafters. Bayfield was always the scene of a good fight. And if you'd dribble too close to the fire escape, the ball would roll all the way down to the first floor.

Pagosa Springs had a balcony over the side line. If you could jump 6'5" to make a basket, you'd hit your head on the bottom of that balcony and knock yourself out.

1946. Silverton was a powerhouse in the San Juan Basin basketball years. Here, the Silverton High School Cheerleaders Connie Arthur, my sister Jean Swanson, Ann Ehrlinger, Gladys Antonelli.

Gerald Swanson collection

SHS Pep Club, 1947. At the Smiley Gymnasium, Durango, Basin B basketball tournament. Cheerleaders are in the center, wearing new uniforms. Jean Swanson is in the center of the picture. The entire town would go to a tournament in those days. You can see the adults up in back. The Pep Club was made up of girls from grades 9-12.

Gerald Swanson collection

SHS Basketball team, 1948. Back row: Coach Harger, Walter "Lags" Gallegos, Don Gray, Kenny Smith, Gerald Swanson, Robert Montoya, Felix Moretti. Seated: Lynn Murray, Richard Maes, Clee Robinson, Don Robinson, Jimmy Drobnick, Mgr. Carl Peterson. The team lost to Burlington, Colo. in the State Semi-finals, Class C Division, by one point.

Gerald Swanson collection

There were a lot of basketball games all over the basin. Our biggest rivals were Ouray, Ridgway and Telluride, mining towns like ours. We had our honor to uphold. Ridgway had a great basketball team. It took all we had to beat them.

After the game, the schools always had a nice lunch for the team. They served sandwiches, lots of punch and cake. There were no such things as Burger King or McDonald's in those days. The sandwiches were usually turkey, ham or roast beef. And they always had lots of homemade doughnuts.

Just for something to do, we used to play basketball even in the summer. We also played touch football—inside, in the gym—in the winter. Spring, we had baseball warmups in the gym. We practiced catch and fielding and batting with nets. It was hard to adapt an outside game to the inside, but with the snow and the winter weather, we learned to do it. Ouray and even Telluride could practice outside, their fields were clear, but ours weren't clear until nearly summer.

Girls didn't have that much to do then. They could be cheerleaders or belong to cheer clubs, but they didn't have teams and team sports the way the boys did. It was all mostly stuff for the boys. Toward the end of the war we did have intramurals, tumbling for girls and boys, gymnastics.

Sophomore year, 1946. Bob Larson, Lynn Murray, Keso (Don) Robinson sitting on top of the shed used to store wood to fire the big ovens of the French Bakery, owned by Lynn's mother.

Gerald Swanson collection

In the spring, we played a lot of baseball with teams from Farmington, Bloomfield and Aztec in New Mexico, and Telluride, Ridgway and Ouray in the mountains.

My junior year, we had an eleven-man touch football league. Silverton played Bayfield, Pagosa, Mancos, and Dolores. We liked it, but it only lasted one year.

There were 250 to 300 kids in SHS then and two basketball teams, twenty boys on each team, grades nine-twelve. There were no competitive sports for grade school, like there are today.

War ends!

A few of the wounded were coming back early, discharged. By 1945, people were anticipating the end of the war. I was a sophomore then. I used to save pictures of airplanes. I was fascinated with them, and probably harbored a secret ambition to be a pilot. There were a lot of stories about the planes and the heroes who flew them. I still have a scrapbook I made during the war years.

I'll always remember VE (Victory in Europe) Day, May 8, 1945, and VJ (Victory in Japan) Day, August 15, 1945. Silverton had one wingding of a celebration! There were a lot of bars in town, all of them with pianos. They hauled all the pianos out into the street, and set up the bars in the street. Drinks were free. It was one vast town of street dances. There were bonfires: people gathered up wood from everybody's back yards, the dump grounds, wherever they could find it. And other people set off dynamite (from the mines) up in the hills.

Uniform service patches, World War II.

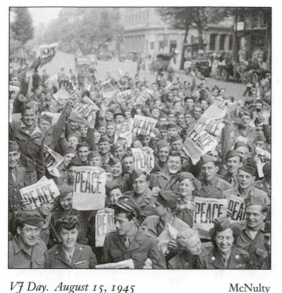

VJ Day. August 15, 1945   McNulty

There were some big celebrations at the Pastime Cafe and Bar (now the Brown Bear) which belonged to my Aunt Rena and her husband, Fidenzio (Phil) Antonelli. The place was a popular hangout, and when people came home from the war, they all went there. A couple of my cousins, Coley Copenhaver and Sylvio (Soapy) Antonelli, had just come down on a furlough. (Both were career men in the service, first in World War II and later in Korea.) Uncle Herman Dalla had just come home, too. So had John Troglia and Joseph Todeschi (who still lives in Silverton, today).

After the war, 1946-1953, Silverton saw a real resurgence. The mines were booming, and railroads were running. A lot of people were back, prospecting and mining. Those were very good years. I graduated in 1948. There was a lot going on in Silverton then, the town was really cranked up.

First date

I was a junior in high school before I had my first date. I took a girl to the junior/senior prom. We went as a group. And we walked; we didn't have automobiles. The girls walked together, the boys walked together. We had to buy the girl a flower. There was a banquet followed by a dance. You danced with different people all night. I only danced with my date once or twice. There was none of this "la-la, ga-ga" falling all over your date bullshit. I had two dates

1947. Howard Hill, me, Lynn Murray, sightseeing at Molas on the way to Durango.

Gerald Swanson collection

when I was a senior, both with Ann Ehrlinger. I took her to a picture show once, then later, to the prom.

First suit

The first suit I ever owned, the first suit-suit, was my junior year. My mother put me on a train to Durango and John Hitti, a friend of Julia Maffey's, met us. He used to work for Mrs. Maffey at the French Bakery in Silverton. Then he worked for the New York Bakery on Main Avenue in Durango, which was owned by Mrs. Maffey from Silverton. Mr. Hitti took us to J.C. Pennys where Lynn Murray and I bought our suits for $19. We both got a grey suit with a little stripe. It was double breasted and had to have the legs tailored to fit. They mailed it to us when it was ready.

I wore that suit three times—to the junior/senior prom for two years, and for my graduation.

We didn't have to worry about buying shoes. My mother took me to Joe Chino's Economy Dry Goods Store (now the burned-out, boarded up building across from City Hall.) We got black shoes, and they hurt my feet so bad I took the damn things off at the prom.

1947. "Kangaroo Court Judges" for freshman initiation week. That's me on the left with Robert Montoya, Billy McGuire and Jack Mulliken. Both Montoya and McGuire are gone now. Montoya retired from the U.S. Air Force. McGuire, who was a great actor, trained in theater at University of Colorado and later worked a variety of jobs. Mulliken, a retired accountant, lives in New York and visits Silverton occasionally.

Gerald Swanson collection

Classmates

There were some real sweethearts, couples, from Silverton School. Lynn Murray and Maxine Cannon were a couple from grade school to graduation. They married in 1951 and they're still married today. My sister Jean and brother-in-law Don Robinson were a couple from grade school to high school too, and they're still married!

My high school graduating class had eighteen people; there were twenty-eight when we started first grade together.

Only three stayed here after graduation: Jimmy David, who was later killed as a miner after the war (his wife Jean still lives here); Mary Moretti Anderson, who was Silverton's County Clerk for years, then moved to Montrose after her husband died; and, me, Gerald Richard Dallavalle Swanson.

1948. Lime Creek. Margie David, Don Robinson, me, Jimmy Drobnick, Maxine Cannon on the way to Durango to the Spanish Trails Fiesta

Gerald Swanson collection

I'm the only one left here now. Eight of us went to college. Six are gone now; twelve are still living—all over the place, in New York, Denver, Arizona, California and Salida. Of my basketball team, between the first and second teams, I'm the only one alive and living here. The other eleven are scattered.

Drama

I did a lot of acting in high school and took drama, because it was an easy elective. I was always looking for the easy way out. In my senior class play, "His Ozark Cousin," I played the lead, Jo Jo Brown. We had a junior and senior class play. We were raising money for stage curtains for the big gym.

We used to have all the plays over there on that stage, years ago. Later I got involved in melodrama in the town and performed in a number of productions here in town.

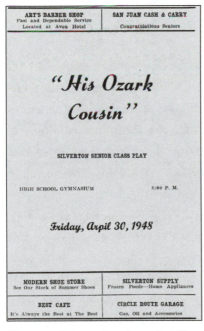

Program from senior class play, June 1948. Notice the sponsors, Modern Shoe Store, Silverton Supply, Best Cafe and Circle Route Garage.

Gerald Swanson collection

Carnivals

Silverton used to have carnivals come to town for Labor Day celebrations. They'd set up on 13th Street, from Greene to Mineral. The three blocks always started at Greene, with a big ferris wheel (set close to where the Pickle Barrel building is now). Next were the lemonade stand and a hamburger stand. The smell was so intense! We never got many hamburgers at home. We'd stand there and watch as the cook would ball up that hamburger, add onions, slap it on the grill.

Sis and I would just stand there and drool. Hamburgers cost ten cents, and of course, we never had any money. So, we'd wait for an uncle to come by (usually it was Angelo), and he'd be good for twenty cents so we could both get one.

1947. Carl Peterson, Ted Hillyard and Lloyd Jones, who fancied himself a cowboy. Labor Day Carnival on 13th Street between Greene and Mineral. The boys won the canes at a concession.

Gerald Swanson collection

1947. Carl Peterson, Ted Hillyard and Lloyd Jones with Gladys Antonelli, attendant for Queen of Silverton, Labor Day Celebration.

Gerald Swanson collection

Next came the carousel. Then a duck shoot, baseball throw, palm reader, genie and the loop-d-loop. The carnival always finished down by Mineral with little cars for little kids to ride in. The cars went 'round and 'round on a track in a circle, and the kids could "drive" them. They also had little airplanes like that.

The carnival ran even during the war. It was an exciting time. It took about two days to set up and ran five days. There were all kinds of games of chance, lots of lights and glitter. It was a big deal for a little mountain town.

Circus

During my school days, we had probably three circuses come to town. It was always the

Clyde Beatty circus, which billed itself as the biggest three-ring circus in the world. Which they weren't, of course, but we didn't know that.

The roads those days were pretty narrow coming up the pass from Durango. They had to walk the elephants along the side of the road to come to town. It always reminded people of Hannibal crossing the Alps with elephants. It was quite a sight to see! One time, they walked two big giraffes down into town, with their trainers. (The circus was held where Silver Summit is today.)

1946. One of three elephants in the Clyde Beatty Circus. The elephants had to walk over the pass from Durango. This picture was taken down by the park, where Red Mountain RV Park is today.
Gerald Swanson collection

A couple of times they brought the ugliest, loudest baboons you'd ever seen or heard. The elephants were mangy, the giraffes pretty old. There were a couple of horse acts, two or three flying trapeze artists, carnival booths and a few dumb clowns that weren't very good.

Even so, we all thought that circus was wonderful. We'd never seen tents that big, that magnificent! The circus really packed in the people. Guys came from Ouray and Durango. People came up even if they had to ride the train.

There was always an adult "men's tent." The sign read, "Come and see the mysterious Egyptian princess dancing the 'Song of the Nile.'" The men and older boys would stand around looking for their wives and girlfriends, hoping they would not see them when they ducked in there. It was mostly belly dancers and stuff. Us kids wanted to go in, naturally. Delmar Pratt, Sammy Maynes, Lynn Murray and I snuck in around back, crawled in so we could look under the tent and see what was going on. Well, when we saw those girls doing that dance, wiggling around like that with very little clothing on, our faces turned red and our eyes nearly popped out of our heads.

Swanson Market delivery truck on Blair Street, 1950 Ford Model F-1. I still made deliveries for my mother's market, but now I could use the truck instead of a wagon!
Gerald Swanson collection

Jean Swanson riding a horse at Lucille Caine's Livery Stable, down on Mineral Street. Jean was Hardrock Holiday Queen's attendant.

Gerald Swanson collection

We jumped up, slid back and ran down over the hill!

When the circus or the carnivals came, they were the talk of town. But, we were glad to see them go, too, to get back to normal. Then we'd sit on the curb by Giacomelli's pool hall...and pine for those hamburgers. Carnival hamburgers! It was the best hamburger I ever ate!

Chautauqua artist

Another kind of entertainment they had when I was in school, they'd get a group of artists under one tent—performers singers and musicians. There might be someone playing the violin, a tap dancer, a magician or maybe someone doing witchcraft. They'd all put on different kinds of acts under one big tent on a vacant lot down where Triangle is today. Every year the town brought a Chautauqua into town. Some of our local writers, artists and musicians would also perform.

The program was a carry over from the old days when Silverton had an Opera House. In fact my home at 1027 Greene Street sits on the foundation of Pascoe's Opera House. Silverton had just about anything the rest of the world had after the train came to town in the late 1800s.

Looking for trouble

We had some good times in junior high and high school. And, as always, we never lacked for ways to get into trouble. One time, when I was in junior high, we started fooling around making carbide bombs. Carbide was what the miner's used in their lamps. You'd put some—it was a white, crystal-like substance—in the lamp, add a little water, and it would make a gas, which you'd light. Anyway, Fatso Gallegos was probably the big instigator for making the bombs. (Fatso was the one with a couple of fingers missing from pounding rocks on the railroad tracks when we were in grade school. He was always doing things like that.) We experimented, put a reasonable amount of carbide in a big fruit jar, added some water and screwed

Don Robinson and classmate Bobby Robinson fake a fight on top of the lean-to roof of the French Bakery. Notice butchers and bakers aprons hung on the clothes line behind them.

Gerald Swanson collection

the lid on tight. Then we sat and waited, maybe five minutes or so, for the gas to build up in the jar. When it was full of gas, we'd shoot it with a BB gun. It would make the most gawd-awful explosion you'd ever heard.

Fatso decided we'd make the bomb of all bombs. He used a gallon glass jug, a good full cup of carbide and a couple of cups of water. We sealed that baby down and put it on "Jew" Fanny's doorstep. ("Jew" Fanny was one of the last of the shady ladies of Blair Street.) We let it work, maybe ten minutes, knocked on "Jew" Fanny's door, then ran around the corner. She opened the door and yelled, "You little SOBs get out of here. Quit botherin' me!"—she knew it was kids you see—and slammed the door. About then, that big old gallon jug blew off all by itself, there was so much pressure in it. It blew out the panel in her door. Good thing she wasn't standing there: we might have killed her!

Another time, I guess it was around the Fourth of July, we were fooling around with dynamite. Kids, grownups too, used to set it off around the Fourth, kind of like fireworks. Clyde Cerniway—he and his dad worked at the Little Dora Mine—came home with some blasting caps and one stick of dynamite. We decided we were going to make the best bomb Silverton had ever heard. We were in our early teens. Clyde was a little older, about 18. We went down there to the curve, where the road turns to go to Durango, and wired a stick of dynamite around a big old spruce tree.

We inserted the blasting cap in the dynamite and strung out thirty feet of black fuse. That stuff burns about a foot a minute. We lit the fuse, jumped over the ridge and ran down past the Little Dora and all the way uptown. Then we sat down in front of Fiore Giacomelli's (where Handlebars is now) so when the thing went off, the cops would see us sitting there and not know we were responsible. The town cop, Mr. Melburg, came by in his green '42 Ford. He was cruising by the Grand Imperial

June, 1947. Summer snow. Fish and Game Department truck in front of Blue Cross Drug Store. I remember sitting in front of the drug store and watching it snow. This started at 10:00 a.m. and by 5:00 p.m. there was twice as much snow.

Gerald Swanson collection

when that baby went off. It echoed all over town—even blew out some windows. We kids were just sittin' there, gigglin' and laughin'. The cop car went roaring down the street, sirens screaming. People in town all went running down there to see what happened.

When the cops came back to town, they came by where we were sitting, innocent as can be. "You little shits know anything about that blast?" Mr. Melburg asked. We said, "No. What happened?"

"Well," the cop said, "somebody just dynamited that big spruce tree down there by the road. There's nothing but a trillion match sticks down there now."

I think he knew we did it, but he never could prove it.

Another time, it was winter, the middle of January, and really hot in our Spanish classroom. The school house was built in 1911 and had steam heat; it could get awful hot upstairs. Well, Richie Maes got up and opened a window. Snow started blowing in, but it cooled down real fast. The teacher, Mrs. Nelson, told him to close the window.

Soon as she wasn't looking, he opened it again. Now, she had him reading at the time, but he'd read and translate in his own dialect. (Richie was Castilian Spanish.) Mrs. Nelson threatened to call Mr. Dunbar, the superintendent. When she went to get him, Richie opened the window, ran around, grabbed all the Spanish books off our desks and flipped them out the window into snow bank. Then he closed the window. Mr. Dunbar made us go out there and dig them up. The teachers and our parents all punished us. We had to miss special events, come in early, stay late and write things like, " I will not throw books out windows," hundreds of times.

One of the best stunts we ever pulled was in chemistry class. We cooked up a concoction with sulphur, which smelled just like rotten eggs. It happened during a break. We took a vent cover off, slipped this smelly stuff up inside, so that when the air started circulating, the odor permeated the whole building with an incredible smell of rotten eggs. Imagine how long it took to run around and locate the source of the smell!

Back then, we weren't bombarded with computers to play with. We had typewriters instead. Now, the best thing about typing was having the girls help us. My friend Lynn

1949. The building where High Noon Hamburgers is today was used as a saloon in the movie "Ticket to Tomahawk," filmed in 1929. Rooms below the "Esmeralda" sign were occupied by "Jew" Fanny.

Don Stott

Murray, for instance, has hands like bananas. His fingers stuck in the keys, and the typewriter would bounce up and down until he could get his fingers out. We all had to take typing, and we all strived to do forty words a minute, without errors. But, most of us never made it. And if we had basketball, a practice or a game, we'd con one of the girls to type our assignments for us and type our names on it. Mary Moretti, Carleen Larson, Helen Loback, Melva Slade—they all used to help us and do that.

Bill Steadman, the pharmacist at Art Lorenzon's drug store, and his wife Marie Steadman, taught science classes at our high school. Some of our gang were a little tough on them, like the incident when we stunk up the school so it smelled like rotten eggs.

We all knew Mrs. Steadman smoked Phillip Morris cigarettes. She used to keep them in the top drawer of her desk in the classroom. When the bell rang and the class dispersed, she'd reach in the drawer, get out a cigarette, then go in the supply cupboard to smoke it. Smoke would curl out under the door, so we knew she was in there.

One day, Richie Maes, Kenny Smith and I were all sitting there. Old Richie says, "Next time Mrs. S. goes out of the room, I'm gonna steal her cigarettes, and I'm gonna smoke 'em."

We had biology class with her later on in the afternoon. Before the bell could ring, Richie lit a PM and blew smoke in the drawer of his desk. It curled up out from

1947. John Mohney, Herman Dalla and Willie Gianetto plowing the "Boiler Slide" in Cunningham Gulch, so guys at the Highland Mary and Pride of the West could get to work.

Gerald Swanson collection

the desk, through the hole where bunson burners used to be. Mrs. Steadman saw it, could smell it and knew one of us had stolen her cigarettes; yet, she never said anything. After class, she called the three of us up front.

"Now gentlemen," she said, "one of you stole my cigarettes."

Richie confessed and said, "You're not supposed to smoke in school."

Mrs. Steadman replied, "Yes, well, I won't tell if you won't tell." So, after that, if one of us wanted a cigarette, she'd give it to us. Even Superintendent Dunbar smoked. It would run out under the door. Some of the teachers even smoked out on the playground.

Graduation

The juniors put on the junior/senior prom for the seniors. They did all the work. In those days, we were very Victorian, everybody was dressed up. The girls in long gowns, the guys in suits. At the dance, we all had little books. We'd write down the girls names for the dances. There was not too much lolly gaggin going on in those days, none of that boy meets girl, kisses all over the floor and up and down the side of the wall. We went in groups to those dances, the boys walked together, the girls walked behind. When we got to the dance, the boys sat on one side, the girls on the other.

The parents helped the junior class cook the graduation dinner. Some of the teachers helped. The dinner was served in the music and activity room. That's where they had home economics, so there were stoves and other stuff for cooking meals. And the English and Drama teachers made sure we had a little course in etiquette—how to use a knife and fork, pour water, coffee. Today we eat like animals,

1948, Senior class photo.

1947. Silverton's baseball team, primarily sponsored by Shenandoah Dives Mine and Mayflower Mill. Some of these guys even played semi-pro or pro ball. Back: Ray Persinger, Lewis Aggis, Ole Olson, Jess Correy, Manager Earl Aggis (in cap), Herman Dalla, Gene Orr, Daryl Aggis (with catcher's mitt). Front: Manuel Garcia, Dick Kantz, Marhsall Floyd. In suit, Billy McGuire, who always kept books, kept score and helped drive the team around.

1948. Below: Silverton's Ball Diamond. Herman Dalla, Ray Persinger and Ole Olson.

Both, Gerald Swanson collection

in front of the TV, out of a box. You have a bunch of people not eating together but eating all over the house.

At the graduation ceremony, the salutatorian and valedictorian both gave an address. There was a lot of competition between them, but both of those addresses were really well done. Some of those kids were outstanding! The salutatorian's speech was ten or fifteen minutes, the valedictorian gave the major address. The superintendent spoke too, and we had a guest speaker, usually

someone from one of the nearby colleges, Fort Lewis, Trinidad or Alamosa. All of them were recruiting for their schools.

Before World War II, there was a lot more recruiting. After that, with the GI bill, the colleges were flooded with returning GI's, guys and gals who wanted to get an education.

Senior trip to Trinidad

That was Trinidad, Colorado, not the island in the Atlantic. We drove down there in Jimmy Drobnick's 1932 sedan. It was an old clunker, but we made it. We all had baseball scholarships to Trinidad Jr. College, so we went down there to look the school over. Well, we looked and weren't too impressed, so we took a walk around to see what we could find. Somebody suggested we should check out the old brewery. It was down by

1948. With my cousin Gladys Antonelli in front of St. Patrick's Catholic Church, Easter Sunday.

Gerald Swanson collection

the Santa Fe tracks. Well, we rang the bell, and pretty soon this little short guy with a great big mustache answered the door.

"What do you young men want?" he asked.

"We came to see the brewery," we said.

Kenny Smith and Clee Robinson, two "drunken amigos" coming out of a bar in Juarez during our senior trip.

Gerald Swanson collection

"Are you eighteen?" he asked. We said we were, of course, so he let us in and we all went to have a beer. There were a lot of little German guys in there. Pretty soon we were feeling good, and the little German guys were feeling good. When we remembered Coach Harger might be looking for us, we went out the back door. The coach found us and asked, "Where have you been?" We told him we'd been out looking around Trinidad.

"You smell like it," he said, and he made us get in the car and start home. We drove most of the way back in silence.

1948. Melva Slade, Clee Robinson, Roberta Montoya, graduating class trip to El Paso, Texas.

Gerald Swanson collection

All we wanted to do was stop every thirty or forty minutes to get rid of some of that beer.

After we got past Salida, Coach Harger said, "I've made up my mind, I won't say anything. I should have been with you and I wasn't."

So he never told we were down in Trinidad drinking beer, and we didn't either. We all had full scholarships—room, board, tuition, the whole thing—but none of us went to Trinidad.

College man

After I came home, my mother decided I was going to St. Regis College in Denver. It was run by the Jesuit priests, who are the world's educators, and my cousin Phil Antonelli was already a student there. All good Catholic boys go to a good Catholic college, and since I was a dutiful son of a little Italian lady, trained to mind my mother—I went!

When it was time to go, my mother packed up just one little cardboard suitcase, with a rope around it, and put me on the Rio Grand Motorway bus in Silverton. We left town at 8 a.m. and got into Denver twelve hours later. The biggest town I had been in before that was Grand Junction.

1948. Lynn Murray, Clee Robinson, Coach Harger, Richie Maes. Photo was taken by Jimmy Drobnick, behind his 1932 Sedan on a class trip to Trinidad, Colorado.

Gerald Swanson collection

1948. Johnny Bonnaventura (right) and my cousin, Phil Antonelli in front of old Silverton Hardware, after the war.

Gerald Swanson collection

I got off at the station at 16th and Stout Street, where there were all kinds of neon and electric lights, and asked someone how to get to the college and they told me to take the street car. He pointed across the street and told me to get on the Number 28 streetcar.

We rode and rode, all the way up to 50th and Federal, where the conductor told me to get off. He pointed to a light and a big building across the street, telling me that was Regis College. Well, it was dark out, and the building looked really big, like something out of a movie, maybe an old European castle.

I walked up and knocked on the big wooden door, and pretty soon it flew open. There was a priest standing there, about five foot tall, bald on top, with a little halo of hair (a tonsure). I showed him my papers that I was supposed to be in the school. He made me wait a long while, then finally had me come in and took me up to the third floor and my room. It was really small, about six foot wide, with two bunks stacked up at one end, two desks, a little dresser, one sink and a toilet. The lighting was pretty dim. It looked like a monastery.

I wasn't too excited at the time, but eventually I grew into it and learned to like it. I also learned to appreciate the Jesuit priests, who were great educators. I went there two years, but by the end of my sophomore year, I was having trouble with one of the laymen teachers, a fellow named John Coyne. He gave me a "D" in my business organization management course, but I'd earned good grades on all my papers and tests. When I confronted him about it, he said, "It's your general attitude in my class. That has a bigger weight. You are uncooperative."

Well, he wasn't a very good teacher, not motivating at all, and I told him so. We had a few words and I stormed out. There was a priest in the hall, and he grabbed me and told me to go back in and apologize. I refused. He said I'd never come back to Regis. I said, "Fine, I'll go somewhere else!"

That fall though, the school called to see when I'd be back. I had to tell my mother what happened. She didn't blame me, and I never went back. I finally ended up going to the University of Colorado and getting a bachelor's degree in science and business and marketing.

I had been on a draft deferment. The day I got my diploma, I got my draft notice and was soon headed for Korea. ✳

1948. Coach Harger. In my senior year, Coach Harger led the Silverton HS basketball team to the championship finals. We played 42 games, and lost only three.
Gerald Swanson collection

✍ Six ✍

Hollywood Comes to Silverton

There were a number of movies made here. One of the first I remember was in 1949, right after I graduated. It was "Ticket to Tomahawk," and starred Dan Dailey, Anne Baxter, Walter Brennan and newcomer, Marilyn Monroe. She played one of the saloon girls. It was her first movie.

"Ticket to Tomahawk"

I was working at the market that summer and got to watch a lot of the action. There were a lot of "Indians" in the movie, real Native Americans, not just actors. They'd come in the store and buy vanilla off the shelves because it was twelve percent alcohol. The movie director, Richard Sale, asked

---

1949. Above: The old National Hall in "Ticket to Tomahawk," one of Marilyn Monroe's first movies.

Below: The locomotive, Emma Sweeny, used in the movie. In the story, the engine was dismantled, brought overland by a twenty-mule team, and on up Blair street to the 'depot" at the town of Epitaph, where it was reassembled.

Both photos, Gerald Swanson collection

my mother Mary not to sell any more vanilla or lemon extract to them because they kept coming in and getting drunk on their breaks!

For some reason, movies were never filmed on Greene Street. They always did the shots on Blair, probably because it was so picturesque. For this one, they brought in a wooden locomotive—it was supposed to be the real one—for the shots up Blair Street to the tracks in front of the depot.

The scenes with Marilyn Monroe playing a dance hall girl were shot at the old National Hall. It was on 12th and Blair and is now a vacant lot across from where the High Noon is now. In the movie, all the dance hall girls were standing on top of the balcony, waving at the train as it pulled into town. (It was the wooden train, though. The real one never did go down Blair Street.)

Above: I wasn't in the movie, but my sister Jean Swanson was. Here she stands in front of the "Marshall's Office" (Hummingbird Shop today) on a wooden sidewalk built for the movie. The building is next to Swanson's Market (today the Dallavalle Inn).

Below: The Emma Sweeney steams away from Epitaph toward Tomahawk, not knowing the bridge ahead has been blown up.

Both photos, Gerald Swanson collection

In the story, the train had to go from Epitaph to Tomahawk, but a competitive railroad company had destroyed part of the track between the two towns and blown up a big bridge over a canyon. Helped by the Indians (a scene shot near Silverton at Molas Lake), the crew and townspeople dismantled the train, loaded it on mule-drawn wagons and hauled it overland to Tomahawk (Silverton).

The movie people used a wooden engine in place of the real one for the dismantling and hauling. It was a whole lot easier to handle!

"Across the Wide Missouri"

This movie was shot in 1951 and I got to be an extra in this one. Most of the scenes were shot around Molas Lake, Little Molas and South Mineral. They didn't shoot any

1951. Mr. Harger, our basketball coach, played a mountain man. His son Tal Harger played an Indian. Tal was several years behind me in school.

Both photos, Gerald Swanson collection

scenes in town. A number were also shot around Haveland Lake, between here and Durango, down at Cascade (where Cascade Village is now) and around Hermosa.

The movie stars were Clark Gable, Ricardo Montalban, Adolphe Menjou and an Indian actress. Our former basketball coach, Mr. Harger, was an extra in the movie, as was his son, Tal, who was in grade school when I was in high school.

Above: Actor James Cagney with Tom Zanoni. Below, right: Paul Beaber (son of newspaper owner) with Bill Vevens, owner of Silverton Motor Lodge (where ZE Supply is now) in front of Swanson's, with the false front made for the movie "Run for Cover."

Both photos, Gerald Swanson collection

"Run for Cover"

Shot during the early 1950s on Blair Street, many of the scenes in this movie took place in front of Swanson's Market while I was cutting meat inside, and many local Silvertonians were extras in the movie. People would be shopping at the market, going in the back door off the alley when they couldn't get in the store through the false-front while movie scenes were being filmed, many of them set against the Hitchin' Post (which used to be a bordello) across the street.

We ran a delivery service those days for people who didn't want to come down the alley to shop for groceries. They

would call their orders in and I'd send out a driver to deliver their groceries right to their home. People in town were excited, it was a big deal. The movie people gave them money for the use of their property, but hell, they didn't want to pay you anything. The extras, and I was one of them, made $10 a day—adult or child. The movie people hired just about every local in town. Lots of people came up from Durango and Ouray, too.

They'd get in line early in the morning to see if any more extras were needed. Those were exhausting days. You'd stand around for hours waiting for the right light or for retakes. There was nothing glamorous about making movies. People needed the work, and they'd show up and wait to see if they could get it.

Tom Zanoni (pictured on the previous page) was born here. Later, he worked in the mines, then went to Fort Lewis College and became a mine inspector. He lives on the Front Range now. His brother, Zeke, is a prime mover in building the San Juan County Historical Mining Museum and in getting the Shenandoah Dives, Mayflower Mill Tour going.

Above: Mrs. Befins with James Cagney, star of "Run for Cover." Left: Actor in the movie with Sandra Voilleque Campuzano, a local Silverton girl who became a business marketing executive.
Both photos, Gerald Swanson collection.

The old Caledonia Boardinghouse restoration at Courthouse Square is one of his projects. Zeke went to Denver, after he married Dorothy and became a fireman, then later he and Dorothy moved back to Silverton. His dad was also a miner and owned the Parlor Ice Cream store on "main" street (in the middle of the block next to Fetch's). I built the fountain in the back. It has two big S's on the top. I was going to call it Swanees. I rebuilt the building, put the front on it, but never could find the time to finish the project, so I sold the building to Zeke Zanoni.

He is also a great photographer, a sculptor, a writer and an artist. Zeke did the designs of the tommyknockers you see around town. He also cast a lot of pewter plates with his photos of locomotives. Dorothy has served as San Juan County Clerk for close to twenty years.

With another Silverton local, John Marshall, Zeke Zanoni co-authored *Mining the Hardrock*, still a popular book today. Zeke and his brother, Tom, helped get the Hardrock Miner's celebrations going here. They also had their own mining museum on "main" street, at the corner of 12th Street, where Tumahawk is today. Tom Zanoni was also a partner in the old San Juan Bar and Cafe. ✳

Seven

Hot Times in Town

I ended up overseas during the Korean War and was stationed in Okinawa, Korea and Formosa. My mother never sent letters, but she would send me the local newspapers and write notes in the margins, all around the edges of the newspapers. The letters were sent to an APO address. Letters like that, they tried to fly them, never put them on the boats.

Okinawa and back

I remember my first Christmas overseas. I received boxes in January and February that were sent the previous November for Christmas. One was filled with cookies, but by the time I got them, there was nothing left but super fine cookie crumbs. One lady sent me fudge, sealed in a tin coffee can with friction tape. I got that about the first of February. It looked pretty good until we opened it, but inside, everything had melted down and was stuck to the sides of the coffee can—it didn't look very appetizing.

I'll always remember, we went shopping up in Toyko for Christmas presents, which we had boxed and shipped home. They assured us the boxes would get home in time for the holidays. They made a very special effort for that, so

Christmas in Okinawa, relaxing after a trip down from the Korean peninsula, 1954. Left to right: Thompson, me, Poules, Young, West. Down in front, O'Hara.

Gerald Swanson collection

Easter 1952. NCO Club, Rhyukas Island, Okinawa. Left to right: Don Moxley, me, Jim Musgrove, Francis Lee

Gerald Swanson collection

I bought a nice assortment of lacquered teakwood bowls. It cost $10, which was a lot of money for those days; I was only making $32 a month. I thought I'd go broke. Well, that stuff went by ship. The ship got in trouble in the China sea. It caught fire and sunk with all of our presents!

I came back from Korea in 1955. Friends met me at the bus depot at the Best Cafe. We walked two doors down to the Club Cafe and Bar, run by Bill Mowat at the time, and had a few drinks. Well, we had a lot of them, I guess. And, I was so taken up with seeing some of my old buddies, that I forgot to go up and say hello to my mother, who had been expecting me. Somebody came in the market and said I was over at the Club Cafe. She came over there and joined us. She was so happy to see me, she didn't scold. "Set 'em up for the boys," she said, and she even had a drink with us. That was quite a surprise, because my mother never drank. She sat there with us for an hour or more. Other people came in and joined us, and when we went back home, arm and arm, she was feeling no pain.

Columbine Tavern

When I got back, I worked for a while at the Columbine Tavern out on the highway as you head north toward Ouray. It was built by my uncle Angelo Dalla and Louis Visintine, who were partners. They started building it back in 1946, hand-mixing the foundation with a little bitty electric mixer. The major timber came from the Silver Lake Tram House. The windows came out of the Stoiber Mill and the flooring out of the Stoiber mansion.

It was a true roadhouse, a beautiful bar. There was a dance floor and a little restaurant where you could always get a good hamburger sandwich cooked by

Uncle Angelo. He served four kinds of beer: Pabst Blue Ribbon, Budweiser, Schlitz and Coors. Schlitz was the favorite beer in Silverton those days, although occasionally a Coors drinker would get lost and come in. There was a live band every weekend. One of the featured groups was Roy's Western Band out of Cortez. They played a lot of cowboy stompin' music. Our favorite was "Minnie the Mermaid." They also played a lot of polkas and waltzes, which Austrians, Italians, Polish and Slavonic people all liked.

On the Columbine's opening night, Angelo and all his relations, including my mother and I, helped out. Angelo took in $2,500, lots of money those days, especially when you consider that beer was 25 cents a bottle. He had so many cars parked in front and down into the road, that traffic was down to one lane. The sheriff had to

1951 in front of the Columbine Tavern. Dobbie Burnell, Louis Visintine, Lydia Copenhaver, "Rocky" the dog held by Angelo Dalla, Phil Antonelli Sr., Coley Copenhaver (married to Aunt Rena Antonelli's daughter Lydia and ???. (Louis was Angelo's partner.) The Columbine was built from material taken out of the old Silver Lake Tram House. The flooring came from the Silver Lake Mansion, the windows from the Silver Lake Mill. The bar was from the old Diamond Belle on Blair Street (not the same Diamond Belle as in the Strater Hotel in Durango).

Gerald Swanson collection

come out and make people move their cars. (You couldn't do it now, everyone would get a DUI. We didn't have DUI's those days. Instead, the sheriff came out, had a drink and led a parade back to town.)

Angelo even ran gambling upstairs during the heydays in the late 1940s and early 1950s. He had blackjack and a 21 table and two

Louis Visintine
Gerald Swanson

crap tables. The gambling was run by a guy named George Brightwell. All the mines were going strong then, the Idarado (Treasury Tunnel), Mayflower, Shenandoah Dives, Pride of the West, Columbus Mine, Kansas City, Highland Mary, Osciola, and Little Dora (at the south end of town).

Angelina worked there. Louis Visintine, Angelo's partner, had gone back to Italy and married her. She had been a cook on the Italian Rivera, and she could make homemade ravioli like you never ate in your life. I bartended there for a while. The other bartenders were Billy McGuire and Sherman Smith (who married my cousin, Gladys, Rena Antonelli's daughter). Saturday night we'd have a fish fry accompanied by lots of good dancin' and lots of good fightin'. Every Saturday night we had to call the sheriff

South of Tony's Bar, the building with the paned windows, was Crippled Mary's liquor store.
Gerald Swanson collection

to break up a fight or haul somebody to jail or restore the peace.

Occasionally there was a domestic fight between a husband and wife trying to kill each other at the bar. One of the best occurred when this husband and wife team, both of them notorious for drinking and battling around town, came in. The wife called

Old Circle Route wrecker. (2002 photo.)
James Burke

her husband a SOB. He knocked her off a bar stool. The wife jumped up, broke a beer bottle and went after her husband with it.

We jumped over the bar and tried to stop it, but that gal just took after us, shouting, "It's none of your business. Let us kill each other." It took three of us, including my Uncle Angelo, Sherman and me to escort them out the door. We threw them out into a snowbank.

Well, they went downtown where they got in a fight at the Benson bar or Club Cafe bar. And, sure as shootin', they were right back at the Columbine the following Saturday.

One time Dr. Holt came in with his girlfriend, Ruth Stofis. It was a cold, snowy night and the bar was jammed. There were a lot of miners in there. The cigarette smoke was so heavy you could cut it with a knife. In walks the doc and Ruth. She comes parading through in high heels and a big long fur coat and yells, "Ladies and gentlemen, I'd like you to see the new fur coat that Dr. Holt bought me." Then she pirouettes, and as she turns around, the coat fell to floor. She didn't have one damn stitch of clothes on underneath. It created a riot. Guys were yellin'. Women were screaming. "Pour me a beer, Angelo," Ruth said. We raced around and found something to cover her with.

That was the same night that I had driven my mother's brand new Plymouth sedan to work. When Doc Holt and Ruth left, he backed his car around and into the

Angelo Dalla was a master high-grader, one of the best in Silverton.
Gerald Swanson collection

side of my mother's car. I was scared to drive home and report what had happened. The next day she took her car down to the Circle Route Garage and said, "Mr. Purcell, you fixa my car and tak'a the bill to Dr. Holt." The body man fixed it and painted it up and sent Doc Holt the bill. I didn't drive my mother's car much any more.

Tall Tales, saloon fights & highgrading

What I always liked about bars in Silverton, when the mines were running, the bars were full of great stories—stories of who found the finest gold, who stole the most gold and silver, and who had the most to sell.

Tremont Saloon Bar

San Juan County Historical Society

My Uncle Angelo was a processor of high- grade ore, a master highgrader. He was so good with his miniature mill, most of the mills wanted to hire him, because of how he could extract the gold out of all the ore. For these endeavors, which were Federal offenses, he served no more than two or three short terms. The last time he was hauled in, his right to sell liquor was taken away. Uncle Angelo was co-owner of the Columbine Bar then, but after that, he couldn't tend bar. So we all tended bar for him.

There were other stories too, especially fishing stories—who caught the most fish at Ice Lake or Clear Lake or Highland Mary's Verde Lakes. Or, who ate the most fish at fish camp. And, of course, who caught the biggest fish. The more the men drank, the bigger the fish got. One little brown trout could grow

Miners rode the tram to and from town.

San Juan County Historical Society

to the size of a wheelbarrow by the end of the evening.

There was a large transient population of "tramp" miners. They'd live in town in rooming houses. And, of course, there was housing for them at the mines. In the old days, you could live up "on the hill" (in a mining boarding facility) for about fifty or seventy-five cents a day, which included bed and board. The food was good, and sometimes you didn't have to go outside at all to get from work to your room. There was a system of caves and tunnels all underground, where the temperature was constant year-round, like at the Sunnyside Mine.

About the only thing you couldn't get up on the hill was whiskey, but the men found a way to smuggle it in.

Sometimes they'd take it up on horseback and stash it somewhere. Others would

Above: ragtime piano player in the Hub Saloon, Grand Imperial Hotel.
Courtesy Grand Imperial Hotel

Left: Old 100 Boarding House.
San Juan County Historical Society

smuggle it in on the trams—the trams took the men and supplies up the hill and brought the ore back down. The trams carried the men down, too, when they wanted to come to town.

One of the first things a lot of them wanted was a haircut, shave and bath. All the barbershops had bath houses. I remember Curtis the Barber and George Bolen's Barbershop. George had three bathtubs at his place. It cost a buck for the haircut and six bits (seventy-five cents) for a bath or a shave. You could get a good bath, a shave, a haircut and a shoeshine for $2.50. The barbershops were originally called Tonsorial Parlors. Many years ago, in the early west, when somebody had a bullet wound, or needed their tonsils taken out, they were taken to the local barbershop. Barbers had scissors, forceps, and—or they thought—limited knowledge of medical training. If barbers had a tendency to get on a good toot and were shaving somebody, they would have to know how to stop the bleeding.

And, of course, the next thing they wanted was a drink of strong whiskey, maybe a woman and, for sure, a chance to gamble their money away. Blair Street was a good place to find all three. The old Tremont Saloon (later the old Bent Elbow, the one Doc Holt burned down) was a popular spot as was Gilheany's Laundry, on the corner of 12th and Blair where the High Noon is now. This one had it all. They had a gambling hall in there, and the reason they called Gilheany's, "The Laundry," was they'd take your money that you'd gambled away in a clean sweep. "I lost my money!" the old miners would say. "They washed it all out of me at The Laundry." The County Club Bar at the Benson Hotel was another hot spot.

The sheepherders used to come in there when they were in town over Labor Day weekend and tie their mules up outside. Once in a while, they'd come out and pass out in the alley. Their money would roll out of their pockets onto the ground. Occasionally one of us would whip up there and grab a quarter. Then we'd go buy candy.

The Anesi family owned the Benson. They had borders, mostly miners, some weekly, some daily. Some of the miners would come in to spend a weekend after having been up on the hill for six months. They normally had a good bankroll. Some of those old miners would stay in the Benson until they ran out of money, then they'd go back up the hill. My Uncle Angelo dealt blackjack and 21. He tended bar there, too. My sister and I always knew when he had a good night, because when we woke up in the morning there'd be a sack of candy there in the kitchen. When he won, it was just like Fourth of July for us.

The County Club had a large bar where the bank is now, gambling, and in the Benson there was also a beauty shop and a liquor store at one time. They even had a meat market in there, which my dad, Irwin Swanson, ran. Also in that building, my uncles Herman and Angelo Dalla had a Conoco garage. The Benson was for adults what Giacomelli's confectionery was for us kids. In the Benson, there was a big kitchen and a big sort-of living room where the guests could sit around. When I was a kid, I used to sit out on the stoop and listen to the honky-tonk piano players. Sometimes we'd pool our nickels so we could buy him a glass of wine.

1960s. The "gunfights" on Blair Street, where the train comes in at 12th and Blair, drew quite a crowd in those days.

Old postcard. Gerald Swanson collection

The Pastime Bar and Cafe (where the Brown Bear is now) was one of the best watering holes in Silverton. All the miners came in there. My Uncle Phil and Aunt Rena Antonelli owned it. Their son, my cousin Phil. Jr., helped run it after he came home from the war (and after his dad died). Rena stayed on until the late 1950s, when she sold the bar to Dean Joseph.

He renamed it the San Juan Bar and ran melodramas in there. Melodrama was very popular then. He put up a big balcony where you walked in the front door, with stairs at the other end, where the kitchen is now. There was a big stage, for the shows. He hired college kids. They had to work in the cafe plus perform in the melo-drama. In return, he provided lodging for them upstairs in a dormitory.

Melodrama and Gunfights

At the same time as Dean Joseph's melodrama, they also had a melodrama at the Bent Elbow and the Grand Hotel. Billy McGuire started the one at the Bent. He had great oleo acts (songs and comedy between the melodrama acts). The place was always packed. There were a lot of tourists, but the mines were running, too. So there was always an overflow crowd in town. Dean's melodrama was really successful.

Dean also did a "gunfight" melodrama out on the street. Dean dressed his girls in bordello costumes. They were also doing a gunfight in front of the Grand Imperial, which was owned by Don Stott at the time. And there was another one down at the Bent Elbow, which was owned by Mike and Effie Andreatta. Well, Dean and Stott got together and decided they didn't want the Bent Elbow to do a gunfight at the train, since it was taking away business from them. So, they decided to have the melodrama gals, dressed in bordello costumes, meet the train. The girls carried placards to lure customers to their places. They tried to interrupt the gunfight put on by the Bent. (The Andreattas had inherited the gunfights from Frank Bostock, from whom they bought the Bent. He had remodeled it and brought in some old buildings from Middleton and Howardsville (now Old Town Square).

Well, friction was building between the Bent, the San Juan Bar and the Grand Imperial. The chefs from the Grand and the Bent got in a fistfight in front of the train's cowcatcher. A few days later, on 12th and Blair where the train comes in, there was another uproar. That same day, the Grand and the San Juan Bar people had their own gun-

Gunfights were fast and furious at the Andreatta's old Bent Elbow on Blair Street.
Gerald Swanson collection

fight up on "main" street. They had a hangman's noose on top of the Indian store. It sounded like a war between Blair Street and Greene Street—guns going off, people yelling and girls screaming. It was the best western you ever saw in your life.

Now, at that time, the city was very poor; we had one city cop, Roy Landcaster. We didn't have any money for deputies, so Don Honeycutt, the representative for Western Colorado Power here, and I (City Councilman and mayor pro-tem at that time) volunteered to serve as deputies. Roy came down to Swanson's Market and said, "Gerald, we're having real a war down here, and we need help." He went and got Don, too, and we both put on our badges. By that time it was a real free-for-all in front of the train. Roy fired off his .38 a couple of times and stopped everything cold. The City Council closed the gunfight down right then.

There was a tour bus in town then, and Don Stott got real vocal, raisin' hell with the bus driver for sending people to the Bent instead of his place. Wilfred "Fats" Downtain, an old Silverton guy, was the bus driver (and he was married to one of the Anesi girls). He told Don to shut up and quit agitating. Don told him to go to hell. Fats picked up a two-by-four and knocked Don to the ground. It's a good thing people were around to stop him, or Fats might have killed him!

It was really a first class free-for-all down on Blair Street at high noon. When the Andreattas ran it, there were always a couple of professional guys that were real good gunslingers. Wiley Carmack (owner of Outdoor World today) was a young business man in town in his twenties then. He was the mortician in the show. It was his job to check all the "dead" guys with a stethoscope while the bodies were loaded into coffins and the gals were wailing and crying. The acting sheriff arrested the bad guys and consoled the gals. There was always one more outlaw who would spring up on the roof and yell. The sheriff blasted him, and the guy fell and dived into a sand lot—he was an acrobat. That would end the gunfight and the crowd would go wild, cheering the good guys and booing the bad guys. Afterward, a couple of banjo players would play music and entertain people. This was all done at high noon on Blair where they had a captive audience when the train came in.

But, after the fracas with Don Stott at the fistfight, after we had stopped the gunfight, we had a City Council meeting that night and voted to suspend the gunfights until a reasonable solution was found. It never was, so the gunfights were shut down. Before long Dean Joseph took out the balcony and the stage at the San Juan Bar. The last melodrama was at the Grand Imperial Hotel. The stage is still there and present owners, George and Debbie Foster, are hoping to resurrect the old melodramas.

Herman Dalla and Charlie Schmalz at the Miner's, September 1982. Charlie ran the mail between Silverton and Delta for 35 years. He also hauled for Meadow Gold Milk.

Gerald Swanson collection

American Legion Bar

Another hot spot in town was the American Legion Post 14 Bar, although it never had melodrama or staged fistfights. (There were plenty of real ones, though.) Aunt Rena ran the bar after she sold the Pastime. She was the legion's first full-time bartender. Before that, members tended bar on a volunteer basis. We moved the bar up front—the area had been a library for the miners—and took all the books, miners' journals and other stuff down to the basement, where there were still some old coffin handles and mortician tables stored from the days when that building was a mortuary.

Where the bar is now, that was the mortuary. It extended out into where the bingo room is now. In the early days, during the flu epidemic, there were so many people dying, they had to stack the corpses (in canvas bags) like cordwood. They put them in the hall in back, where they dance now.

The Legion Bar was supposed to be private, for members only, but Aunt Rena would let anybody have a drink that wanted one. We got challenged on that a lot of times, and shut down more than once because of it.

My Uncle Herman started helping her, running the bar at night. Eventually he took over as the Legion's second full-time bartender. Guys would get off the swing shift or early shift and come down to the bar for a beer. All the mine buses stopped in front. Guys would come in with their pie cans and muddy boots. In the winter,

Miner's Union Hall, American Legion Post #14 (2002 photo).   © Kathryn Retzler

the place got pretty muddy, what with the ice melting off their boots. Herman had to mop several times a day.

Billy Rhoades was the bartender for a while after Herman. Billy was a couple of years ahead of me in school, a great athlete, basketball and baseball player. Everybody wanted him on the team. He graduated from Ridgway High School, and I remember when we had to go over there and play them. He was a very competitive player. After school he mined, he mined all of his life—forty-five years—and

worked at least fourteen mines. The last ones he worked for, before taking over as the manager at the Legion, were the American Tunnel and the Sunnyside. "Lord, I love mining," Billy would say.

His wife, Fadona, was the postmistress here for thirty-five years, and his daughter works there now.

To this day, the legion bar still has the "Round Table" up front. It's the closest table to the door, and the first place the miners went when they came in off shift and wanted a cold beer. Their wives might join them, sitting up on the

Billy Rhoades
Gerald Swanson collection

"Round Table" at the Miner's Tavern. Ernie Kuhlman, Mark Lee, John Ross, Ted Toms (Legion Commander), Bill Taylor (manager) and James Burke. (2002 photo.)

Kathryn Retzler

radiator where they could warm their butts. That table used to be a gaming table, and originally came from Jack Gilheany's gambling saloon. There's a slot to drop money in, "cartwheels" (dollars) and chips. Sometimes there'd be as many as ten or twelve guys sitting there—in my days, guys like Patrick Willis, Paul Woggon, Pete McDonald and Fred Anderson. I was an adjutant of the American Legion here for thirty-five years and spent some time at that round table. The Legion is still a good local neighborhood bar—and it's open to the public now. In fact, it's the only real neighborhood bar in Silverton.

The Arcade used to be a pool and beer hall. They served extra-hot chili con carne and homemade tamales, too.

Gerald Swanson collection

Café crowd

When I was growing up, there were a lot of restaurants around town. The American Cafe, in the Grand Hotel, was run by George and Jinks Sitter. (George was the guy who didn't like to cook hamburgers. He was also the town judge.) The Club Cafe and Bar on "main" street, Fetch's building today, was run by Bill and Svea Mowat. This is where Jess Carey cooked, the guy that made all the Thanksgiving turkeys, and when nobody ate them, he threw them all in the trash can and walked out.

We also had a little place called the Miner's Diner where the funnel cakes place is today. That was run by Nora Bolen (wife of George the barber). She was a great old-style cook, and she made wonderful pies. After she quit, a guy named George Tarcia moved in there and started a diner. He always said he'd serve any kind of soup you wanted. If you came in and ordered a bowl of bean soup, for example, he'd say, "Just a minute."

Then he'd run out the back, run over to the French Bakery, buy some Heinz bean soup, cook it up and serve it. We used to sit and watch him cook hamburgers over his grill. He always had a cigarette with a long ash hanging out of his mouth. We'd wait for it to fall off and land in the grill!

The old Best Cafe, where Silverton Mineral's and Gifts is today, was run by the Giacomelli family, who had a lot of bar and restaurant businesses in town. (Amelia Daily bought the lot after the old building had caved in from a snowstorm.) There was a period of time when it was run by an eccentric alcoholic. He'd come over and ask me how much beef I had. I'd show him, sell it to him and we'd take it over there in my truck. He always paid in cash. He'd get on a big drunk, and he'd decide to remodel the Best Cafe, haul all the booths and tables out on the sidewalk and stack them up and proceed to paint the floor or something. If he got mad at the customers, he'd turn up the juke box, put up the "closed" sign, sit on the stoop and drink whiskey, turning everybody away.

One time he came in to see my mother and said, "Mary, I know you're a Catholic, and I want to talk to the Pope. And if I can't talk to the Pope, by God, I'll talk to his wife."

The first time they painted the double yellow line on "main" street, he thought that was so neat, he went out and laid down and took a picture of those lines.

We also had a restaurant, the Arcade (still the same name today). They sold 3.2 beer, hot dogs, two or three kinds of sandwiches plus an extra-hot chili con carne and homemade tamales. It was run by a gal named Mattie McDonald. She did very well there. Mattie had originally bought the old Club Cafe. A guy named Petley came along and offered Mattie five thousand dollars for it. She sold, and he put in a big gift shop and made postcards which he sold all over the area. There was a gal, Ann Tomasi (married to George Tomasi, a local Silverton boy), who ran that gift shop over there for twenty years for Petley. So, the Arcade has been a gift shop for more than forty years.

A lot of the bars had food, mostly soups and stews. There were no such thing as hamburger stands, except when carnivals came to town. Most bars and restaurants cooked hamburger sandwiches. A few had french fries, but mostly they just served mashed potatoes. Most restaurants catered to the working miners and traveling people. We didn't have a lot of tourist-type public restaurants, because many miners lived in boardinghouses, which furnished their meals or they had their own homes. It was not like today, where the whole family jumps in the car and goes out to eat.

When I was a kid, a miner made $5 to $7 an hour, good money in those days. A T-bone steak cost a buck twenty-five ($1.25). You could get a good hamburger at the American Cafe (if George Sitter would make it for you) for twenty-five cents and a big bowl of mashed potatoes and gravy for another nickel. A glass of milk also cost a nickel. You could get a cup of coffee and a piece of pie for twenty-five cents

Gold King Mill, Gladstone. People from Silverton rode up to Gladstone on the Silverton Northern to attend dances at the community hall in Gladstone. The train ran into the 1930s.

San Juan County Historical Society

those days. (And, it was a piece of pie, not a little bitty half inch slice.) Beef roast cost nineteen cents a pound at our market. So, you could feed four or five people at home for the same price as one meal in a restaurant.

Dances

It was a treat for me to go out after a dance and have pie á la mode with a glass of milk or an orange Nehi soda. We always used to go to a restaurant after a dance, although mostly it was the adults who would go out for breakfast. When I was growing up, they stayed open after the dances, sometimes until four in the morning. They usually served one set thing—fried eggs, ham, potatoes and toast.

Dances usually started around 9:00 p.m. and didn't quit until 2:00 a.m. The bars stayed open that late, too. People loved to dance. I grew up in a dance era, an era of great music. We had some great bands in this town, all locals. Man they were good. Some of the bands used to play around the old boardinghouses for the miners. Musicians came to town, worked the mines, offices and dance halls, playing piano in the dance halls. They came from all over the world. There were brass bands, too.

We had everything. I remember an orchestra called Ernie Anderson, from Durango. They had ten people in that band. Old Ernie was completely blind, but he could play the piano really well. There wasn't a song he couldn't play. He reminded you of the great pianist, Eddy Duchin.

The Miner's Union Hall was the biggest dance hall in Silverton. (Presently A Theatre Group uses that space.) It was a real classy dance hall. The floor, white oak, was buffed clean. (When it wasn't used as a dance hall, it was a meeting hall for the union.) They had a big canvas tarp to cover the floor, which they took up when there was a dance. There were beautiful light fixtures, lovely benches around the sides, and fans—it was the only place in town that had fans. When a lot of people were dancing, the heat got terrific in there. The bandstand was on the "main" street side of the building. I remember going there with my mother and sister when I was a little boy. When we got tired, we'd go in the anti-room where the old ladies would watch us while we slept. Everyone was dressed up, the women in long dresses, the men in suits and ties, the miners fresh from the bath houses, cleanly shaven with their shoes shined. It was an era of elegance. You never saw anyone at a dance in those days in jeans or dungarees—or as they used to call them, "slobs." We had class, formal dances, ball room dancing and nice clothes. Although at the saloon dances, you could wear hobnail boots if you wanted and if they would let you...maybe.

Dances were a great form of town entertainment. When you put together so many people, so much whiskey and beer, you saw some of the best fistfights this town ever saw. It was "knock 'em down and roll 'em down the steps." The cops would be waiting at the bottom to grab them and haul them off to jail.

Johnny Jenkins was one of the best of the saloon fighters. He was short and wiry, a local miner, and he was also a great dancer. He used to promenade around the City Hall dance floor with his wife, Louise Jenkins. His daughter, Thelma "Tootsie" Jenkins, lives in Montrose now. He was also involved in the local badger fights in Silverton and in Eureka.

Eureka was before my time, but my mother told me about the great dances they used to have up there at the community hall and the old boardinghouses. The Sunnyside ore processing mill was working thirty or forty years up there, and people from Silverton would go up on the train, stay until the dance was over, then ride back to town. The train stopped right at the community hall. Sometimes the Silverton people, all decked out in their finery, would ride up in the ore buckets for a dinner and dance at one of the boardinghouses. Imagine a lady riding up with a nice coiffure, the warmest coat she owned, high button shoes and a big blanket. She'd go up on the Silverton Northern Train, then switch to an ore bucket for the last leg of the ride.

The last train to Eureka was in 1938. It ran until the Sunnyside shut down, and the town along with it. The rails came up in 1944 to 1945 for scrap for the war effort. In my mother's day, the trains went clear up to Cunningham Gulch and Animas Forks. Another branch went up to Gladstone to the Gold King and the Gold Prince. Gladstone started going down in the early 1930s, although ten years before there had been some disastrous fires up there.

Badger Fights

Eureka and its community hall were also the home for some of the greatest badger fights in Western Slope history. Now these badger fights were unique to the area, a special treat. And illegal as hell. Sometimes, when the sheriff or the game warden, if either were new to the area and didn't know what was going on, got wind that one was about to happen, he'd show up, threaten to arrest everybody. (Although, other times, he might be a participant, or one of the guys betting on the outcome.) I remember when we had a new, young State Game Warden. He showed up one time with warrants for our arrest and warrants to serve on the city and commissioners for

violation of cruelty to animals, dogs, sensitivity and emotions of human beings.

I think badger fights were probably dreamed up by early-day miners for something to do. It was outlandish in some people's eyes, entertaining to others. People would gather at the fight place, up at the Eureka Community Hall in the old days, the

Ross Beaber, Silverton Standard *publisher, and Johnny Jenkins, a local mining character, stand in the doorway to the Miner's Union Hall, where badger fights were held.*

Gerald Swanson collection

Left: Charlie Wing and Ed Koltz help badger fight participant (dog protector) suit up before the event. His cardboard "armor" is taped on with friction tape. The leg protectors are made from the bottom of heavy steel carbide cans (which had contained carbide for the miners' lamps).

Right: One of the famous, strong-willed badger fighters volunteered to help protect the dog when the badger charged out of the barrel. Usually this guy was one who was very vocal around town, a "know-it-all," frequently a newcomer and a genuine braggart who was willing to protect the dog against the gnashing bicuspids of the ferocious wild badger.

Both photos, Gerald Swanson collection

Miner's Union Hall in my day, and prepare for the fight. There would be a lot of excitement and taking sides. And betting, of course. Men and women both came. Sometimes the kids, too. Guys would train their dogs all year to be "badger fighters." We'd pick some new guy to town, usually a loudmouth, cocky guy, as the "patsy" for this event, the "dog protector," and tell him how dangerous it would be. He'd have to be all suited up for protection in heavy cowboy chaps, cardboard or other "body armor," a baseball catchers mask, oven mitts, tin cans on his shins or his head—anything outlandishly goofy. Before the fight, he'd throw his weight around and brag, "I can fight that badger."

Above: Suited up and ready to fight! Jimmy Baudino, Ross Beaber, ?, Claude Deering, Bud Bertram, Uncle Louis Dalla.

Below left: Roy Roff (probably Silverton Town Marshall at the time) beats on drum end of barrel to calm down badger while Wallace Purcell helps hold barrel to keep badger from turning it over.

Below, right: Frank Giacomelli with his favorite badger-fighting dog, Black Night.

All photos, Gerald Swanson collection

While the men thumped on a barrel, people would climb up on the risers, in case the badger jumped out. Floor guards, "crowd control people," would circulate around. Others were ready with revolvers, in case the badger got away and ran wild. Badgers can be pretty mean, really dangerous. There were "agitators" on the floor, whose job it was to protect the dogs. Or, if a badger went wild, to try

Postmaster Frank Salfisberg (left) presents Ross Beaber (right) with commemorative plaque honoring Silverton's badger fights. Johnny Jenkins is in the middle.

Gerald Swanson collection

to grab the dog and take him to safety. There would be a number of women in the crowd, crying, wailing, screaming, protesting the cruel treatment of badgers and dogs. They were shills, some of these guys' wives. The whole thing was a massive performance. Some of these people were really good participants! And someday, maybe we can renew the badger fights. ✳

Claude Deering, long-time Silverton resident, comments on badger trophy to Frank Salfisberg, then the local postmaster. Frank is looking straight at the audience, wanting to impress upon their minds the importance of the famous badger fights. Because there was so much money wagered on badgers, and betting was part of this program, probably he represents the anti-badger fighting collation, there to stop so-called "inhumane" game of pitting dogs against badgers, just as there have always been folks opposed to cockfights.

Gerald Swanson collection

✂ Eight ✂

Fourth of July

July Fourth has always been a big day in Silverton. In the old mining days, it was one of two days the men had off. (The other was Christmas.) We still go all out for celebration of that day, especially with our parade, which is the best on the Western Slope! I've been Parade Marshall a number of times, and, almost always, I've been in the parade, too.

The big event, besides the parade, is the water fight, a tradition that goes back to when neighboring fire departments competed to see who was best with hoses and fire equipment. In the real old days they had hand-pumpers (on a horse-drawn wagon) and buckets. Now it's fire trucks and high-pressure hoses, and everyone gets wet before the contest is over.

The day includes other events such as a fun run, contests and a street dance. At the park, folks gather for band concerts and an ice cream social.

1985. I'm on the left, Al Homann is on the right, and that's Richard Baca's 1956 Caddie. We were "Protectors of the Shady Ladies" in this year's parade.

Gerald Swanson collection

1980. Silverton's famous Brass Band puts on a concert in the park (and around town) and marches in the parade. Pictured here, front: Allen Nossaman, Todd Chapman; Middle: Terry Morris, ?, Janet Sharpe, Dennis Kurtz, Kathy Gardner; Back: Jerry Hoffer, Gary Miller, myself, Dale Meyers, Tom Tesh.
Above, Tommy Wipf. All other photos, both pages, Gerald Swanson collection

Left: "Alfred Packer Dining Club Walking Exhibit." That's me with the wheelbarrow.
Next page, top Right: Tom Savich with a "bootleg still on wheels."
Bottom right: Don Stott represents the "Oklahoma Sooners headed West."
Far right: With Uncle Herman in uniform.

Above: little kids parade down the street on a rainy July 4th.

Middle: Richard Baca driving his old Caddie. In back, me, John Crispen, Al Homann and "the girls."

Bottom: 1980 American Legion float with WWII Army command car passes Swanee's Candy store (now the Villa Dallavalle). Andy Hanahan is driving and Uncle Herman is sitting next to him in the front seat. I'm in the back with Lynn Murray.

All, Gerald Swanson collection

4th generation Dallavalles. Casey Dowling (grandson of Jean Swanson Robinson), Taylor Thomas (Nancy's granddaughter), Kelsey Brown, Bryson Thomas, Kelly Noon (Judy Swanson Noon's son) as Superman.

Left: 1984. Me with Uncle Fury Dalla.

Below, 1976. Colorado Secretary of State (far left, her husband far right). Herman Dalla wearing his father's top hat and high-grade gold chain, me, in my mayor's coat.

Gerald Swanson collection

Above: Taylor Thomas (Nancy's granddaughter) and friend Kelsey Brown riding in back. Peeking from balloons, Bryson Thomas, Taylor's brother. Passenger "Superman" Kelly Noon (Judy Swanson Noon's son). Geri Swanson is in the driver's seat!

Left: Me as "Jack the Giant" wearing my rhubarb costume. All my daughters also wore rhubarb costumes, and we were the winning entry that year. (1980s)

(Our entire family usually got dressed up and participated in the July 4th parades, and we frequently won the prize for best theme.)

Below: Leading the Irish coalition in 1992. John Wright is leading the American Legion Unit, following the colors.

Gerald Swanson collection

Nine

The Political Years

After I was discharged from the service, I came back to Silverton. I was just going to stay a few months, get my feet on the ground, then I was going to go to Silverton, Ohio and work with General Electric. A senior executive officer I had met in the service offered me a job there when I told him I had a degree in marketing.

Meantime, I came back to town and started settling down, visiting at my Uncle's Columbine Tavern, doing the bar bit with the boys and helping my mother out at Swanson's Market. Finally, my mother said, "Gerald, you know I really need a meat cutter." (There was nobody around to help her cut meat.) "Why don't you learn something about it," she said. So, I said, "All right, I'll just try it for a while." I went down to the Callaway Packing Plant—they were in Olathe then—and talked to Buzz Callaway. We got to visiting, had a few drinks together, and he suggested I come down and work in the plant for a month or so to get a hands-on education in meat cutting. I'd go down and stay ten days or a week, then come home to Silverton. He broke me in on primal cuts, where to cut, how not to cut, how to break carcasses down, how to grade the meat. After four or five months, Buzz said I should give it a try and he'd help me anyway he could, when I needed it.

Swanson's Market   Gerald Swanson collection

So I became a meat cutter, and I continued doing it for more than forty years, working alongside my mother at the market and eventually running the market myself.

Settling down with Stela

Maria Stela Leitao Swanson

Every Sunday, I went to the Catholic Church with my mother. One particular Sunday, I looked over and saw a very pretty girl sitting on the other side of the church. I asked my mother who she was, and my mother said, "That's Maria Stela Leitao. She teaches languages at the school."

Stela was very classy looking, Portuguese, and she spoke English and French: she taught both languages in school. Stela, who was in her second year of teaching in Silverton, was also the senior class sponsor and Pep Club Sponsor. That was in 1955, and the starting wage those days for a teacher was $2500 a year.

June 10, 1956. Gerald Swanson and Stela Leitao wedding, St. Patrick's Church. My attendant and best man, Herman Dalla, Carl Longstrom, Thomas Savich, Phil Antonelli. Stela's attendants included Laura McCarrier and Gloria Woods.

Gerald Swanson collection

1956. Mary Swanson and Stela Swanson. (Building in background, on left behind Mary, is Giacomelli's, now Pickel Barrel.)

Gerald Swanson collection

After church that day, my mother introduced me. It was in the fall, and the colors were turning; I asked Stela if she'd like to take a picnic and see the fall colors. She got in our 1950 Ford pickup and we drove around, then went up to South Molas and stopped by a stream for our picnic. You know how it is when you meet somebody new. You start exchanging things about your lives. I came to find out she was a graduate of Loretto Heights College in Denver, a women's college, and was there about the same time I was at Regis College. I also found out she was born in China. Her dad had worked for an American import/export company in Shanghai. At the time, her family lived in Macau, a Portuguese colony. They were run out of China by the communists. She, her parents and her oldest brother and a sister left. Another brother was working in Brazil at the time.

Anyway, Stela and I got together. We didn't date heavily. We'd go bowling at Giacomelli's (where the Handlebars is now) or go to a picture show at the Lode Theater. (They had movies on Wednesday, Friday and Sunday.) Because she was teaching and had to be up early for school, Stela never stayed out past 9:00 p.m.

The following Christmas, I had to go to Denver to be best man at my cousin Phil Antonelli's wedding. Stela had plans to go to Denver to stay with old friends who had been in China with her and her family. So we both went, and we had a great time. I included Stela in my itinerary. After we got back we went together off and on. Then the love bug hit me and we got engaged in the winter of 1955. All thoughts of ever moving to Silverton, Ohio hit the tubes.

We were married June 10, 1956. I was working full time with my mother in the grocery store. Stela and I started having children and became more entrenched in

June 10, 1953. My sister, Jean Swanson, married Don Robinson at St. Patrick's Church. Best man was Don's brother, Clee Robinson. Others in the wedding party include Don Stott, "sister" Anesi, Phil Antonelli, Gloria Woods, Jimmy Baudino, Gladys Antonelli, Sherman Smith and me (upper right). The two little girls are Laura Lee Baudino and Becky Todeschi.

Gerald Swanson collection

the community. We ended up with five children and a nice little grocery and meat market business. which continued into the 1980s.

Introduction to politics

I had joined the Rotary Club in 1956, before I was married. Ross Beaber was president at the time. He recruited me, but I was at that age where most of the members were twenty years older than me. So, I became prime mover to charter a Lions Club in Silverton. Montrose and Durango Lions became

 charter partners. We started with sixty-five members, most of them younger men. We had some great programs—eyeglasses for children, operations for kids' eyes, ears, nose, throat, any kind of medical need.

As time went on, I got to dabbling in Republican politics. My old-time friend, Art Lorenzon, who had been the

Ross Beaber, Silverton Standard publisher, was active in the Rotary Club.

Republican party chairman for many years, asked me to serve as vice chairman. At the time, my mother was a Republican and my Uncle Louis was the Republican County Commissioner. The Democratic Commissioner, Phil McClosky, was up for re-election. Art decided to run against Phil for County Commissioner. We all told Art, "Don't do it." He had been Republican Chairman for too long and had made some enemies. Well, he ran anyway, and ran a heavy, hard campaign. But poor old Art lost his bid to Phil. It kind of blew him out. He quit as Republican County Chairman, saying, "Swanson, you're going to have to take over. It's time for me to quit. They wouldn't put me in as commissioner, so I don't want to be the chairman anymore." That loss took the wind out of his sails. Art was born in Silverton. McClosky was a transplant—but a smoother talker.

Donkeys vs Elephants

So, I got all entwined in the Republican Party. But, I had to come up against L.W. Purcell, and he had been Democratic County Chairman since 1910. Lew knew more about politics than most people learn in a lifetime. When I took over as Republican Chairman, he said, "Congratulations young man, I'll show you all you need to know."

For many years he and I locked horns on candidates. I'll always remember, Uncle Herman ran for county commissioner after Uncle Louis finished his term.

When the campaign started, Lew announced, "I'm gonna go out and get him! And we'll give you a good fight." Against Uncle Herman, Lew ran Bob Ward, who was county sheriff at the time and a mining engineer.

Well, the first ad I put in the local paper read, "We like Bob Ward, but we love Uncle Herman because he's our uncle and we want you to vote for him." Signed the Swanson kids, Judy, David, Janet, Claudia and Geraldine.

Everybody got a kick out of that. The campaign got to be pretty heavy, but Uncle Herman won. So, I got one up on old Lew there. Over the years, there were numerous political battles, but we all had a common ground—if we had a particular individual who was doing a good job (coroner, treasurer, etc.), with the exception of county commissioners, we always fought on that. In those days, politics was a lot of fun and had a lot of local flair. We used to set up a Republican headquarters and a Democratic headquarters. Each one had a little bar inside. The week before election, people would stop by for a cup of coffee—or a drink. We always had plenty of wine, plenty of whiskey. You might say we were

My Uncle Louis was Republican County Commissioner when he first got into politics.

Gerald Swanson collection

buying votes. We used to meet the mine crews as they came off their shift. We had a bottle of booze with us. We'd stop the mine bus at the end of town. Uncle Louis and Uncle Herman would get on the bus and pass the bottle. "Here José, here Joe, have a drink on us!" It was fun.

We had a number of old-timers in town who were schooled in the art of getting a drink for free. Remember Ben Bagozzi (the guy who cooked his stew in a pressure cooker and blew himself right out of his house)? Well, he'd come in whichever headquarters and announce, "This election, I'm going to vote straight Republican." Then, he'd ask, "You don't happen to have any whiskey do you?"

Vote for Uncle Herman

He'd drink some, then wander across the street and say the same thing to Lew at the Democratic head-quarters. Now, on election day all the bars are closed, but at headquarters, you could get whiskey. Sometimes those old-timers never did make it to the polls. One of the biggest violators was Art Lorenzon himself. He'd be passed out back there, on a chair, when the polls closed. We'd pour water on him, start pouring coffee down him, so he would be awake for election results.

1956. Man about town!
Gerald Swanson collection

We didn't have computers those days. We weren't allowed phone calls to check on results. It was against election rules to call outside of the office to find out (or tell someone else) how the vote was going. To get around it, we had runners. My cousin Clyde Todeschi and I were runners. We'd go to both polling places, the first and second precinct, where we'd get a slip with names of the people who had voted. We'd come back to our headquarters and scratch those people's names off the voting list. As the day wore on, if it looked like votes were not coming in, we'd get on the phone and call the people who hadn't voted yet. We'd offer them a ride to go vote. About 4:00 p.m. every afternoon, we started an underground pipeline. The gals in the counting room would go to the bathroom, take a little note saying something like, "Louis Dalla is ahead by ten votes." They'd hide the note in the rest room. If our guy was falling behind, we'd go out and get more people to vote. Ingenious, wasn't it?

In the old days, they even did better than that. My mother said, years ago, they'd go up to Howardsville to pick up the votes. They'd have a wagon ready, with votes for their man, and switch boxes of votes, so their man won.

San Juan County for many years was mostly Democrat, when the rest of Colorado was Republican. (San Juan

Fishing at Molas Lake. That's a brand new 1956 Plymouth Belvedere in the background. The license plate says "55," which was San Juan County's state ranking. We were the sixth smallest county in the state.
Gerald Swanson collection

County used to go the opposite most of the time. People here just liked to be contrary.)

There were many fistfights on election days. Usually it resulted in the younger Republicans and younger Democrats debating candidates in front of one of the headquarters. They didn't debate environmental programs or social status. Politics was more cut and dried. Cut the taxes, raise the taxes. Voters didn't care who the guy was sleeping with. Now they dig up all the dirt. Back then people cared more about the issues.

In my time, we didn't have television, we couldn't see results on TV. Radios weren't worth a damn. So you had to wait until you got phone calls, say from the state headquarters in Denver, to see how

4th of July, 1979. Standing, Lew Purcell, Democratic Party Chairman, who was named "Citizen of the Year." Seated behind him is Fenrick Sutherland, retired Social Services Dept. Director for San Juan County.

Gerald Swanson collection

votes tallied. We didn't work on percentages like we do now, where the guy winning the popular vote doesn't necessarily win the election. It might be noon the following day before you knew who was President or State Governor. Also, campaigns weren't so

1968. Mary Dallavalle Swanson behind the counter of Swanson's Grocery and Market where she spent from 1941 to 1985. She is sixty-six years old here and not one grey hair! My mother loved candy (see the candy bars behind her and over her head). Every afternoon she'd turn around, look at the candy, select a candy bar and eat it. She worked forty-four years in this building her parents built in 1901.

Gerald Swanson collection

The Swansons, 1966. Back: Janet and David. Middle: Stela and me. Front: Claudia, Geri and Judy.

Gerald Swanson collection

dirty; we didn't spend the same kind of money we do today. We did have scandal, but it was mostly confined to a particular area, and it took days for scandal to cross the country, maybe by telegraph.

Serving in Silverton

Republican County Chairman— I served in that position for thirty-five years. Overall, I had more fun doing this than just about anything else. We used to pull pranks on each other all the time. Lew (L.W.) Purcell and I used to set each other up. We'd plan a joint Rotary and Lions Club meeting. Lew was a charter Rotary member, so we'd have the meeting at The Grand Imperial Hotel. Lew ran the hotel at the time. He really ran a tremendous hotel.

When we were having a meeting there, I'd go in and say to Merv Magneson, the bartender, "Lew told me to tell you to set the bar up and charge it to him." Those days a highball or shot of booze was just seventy-five cents. Now, if you had sixty couples there, and half of them drank, it was a pretty good bill. Then somebody else would tell Magneson the same thing. I remember one night, they'd charged three rounds to L.W. Next day he calls me up, says, "Come by the hotel after you get out of the shop." I'd go,

We held joint Rotary/Lion Club meetings at the Grand Imperial Hotel.

San Juan County Historical Society

and he'd stand there, shaking his finger. "You sly son of a bitch," he'd say. "You got me good."

We also had bubblegum contests. You'd chew it up and spit the gum into an empty beer glass on the floor. We'd see who could do it the fastest and get it in that glass. Okay, it was silly, but when you're half drunk, you do all kinds of things.

One time we had visiting Lions and visiting Rotarians from Durango and Montrose. There were about 140 people in the room. The meal was turkey. The waiters were going around, serving everybody. Lew was watching carefully, and when they got to me, he laughed like hell. He'd had his cook fix me a plate with two slices of raw turkey, and I mean completely raw, with two hardboiled eggs underneath and hot gravy poured all over the top of it, so it looked like some kind of Louisiana hot sauce on top. Well, I took a big bite and then spit it right back out. The eggs stunk, the hot sauce burned my mouth and the turkey was rubbery and raw.

During that period of time—I was in my forties then—when the Best Cafe was running up here, every morning at ten and every afternoon, we'd have a coffee hour. Business men would go over there and flip for who was going to buy coffee. Once

1981, Durango. Ribbon cutting to celebrate new owner of D&SNGRR Charlie Bradwhaw (center) with Durango Mayor Robert Hatfield. Silverton's present mayor, Ernie Kuhlman, still wears the same blue frock coat I'm wearing here. He got it from Al Holmann, who I gave it to. Ernie said, "Don't ever get rid of that coat. Only the best people have worn it. If you have to, encase it in mothballs, but save it!"
                                                                    Gerald Swanson collection

Greeting people as Mayor of Silverton on Charlie Bradshaw's special train. That's Colorado Governor Dick Lamm on the left. As the mines closed down, the railroad and the visitors it brought daily to Silverton, had and still has a major impact on Silverton's economy. Instead of bringing in supplies for the mines and the town, the train now brings hundreds of thousands of tourists to town every season.

Gerald Swanson collection

in a while we'd all gang up on somebody else, like Phil McClosky. Somehow, he always wound up having to pay for the coffee. It finally dawned on him something was going on. Lew had made up some special coins, some with both sides heads, some others with both sides tails. He'd make like he was flipping one of those coins, and when Phil said "Heads!" Phil would drop the tails coin. We were a lot more mischievous when we were younger.

Town Council—I served there for a number of years, too. One time we had a doctor out of Denver, a dentist, who come up and spoke to us about putting fluoride in the city water. A lot of the kids had bad teeth, and this guy advocated getting state aid to improve the water. The doctor gave a good presentation, which was well received. But the whole time he was talking, he was also smoking his pipe. Everybody smoked then, the room was full of smoke. Don Stott, who owned the Grand Imperial at the time (the guy who had been in the fistfights when the Bent Elbow and the Grand Imperial were competing for the best tourist-show gunfights in town) got up and started to object. He could be really obnoxious. He stood up and said, "How can this guy be for fluoridating the water or anything about good health when he's standing there, smoking that stinky pipe and smoking up my lungs."

Stott kept pestering the doctor, ranting and raving, really carrying on. I told Bob Baca, the city policeman, to take him outside and not let him back in. We apologized to the doctor.

The state put the fluoride in, but people didn't do a good job of maintaining it, so that program went right down the hill.

Silverton School Board—I served ten years on that board, four of them as president of the board. I think positions on the school board and the city council bring out the worst in people. Sometimes you're forced into saying things you probably shouldn't say, and sometimes,

Colorado Governor Lamm greets passengers who rode the train up from Durango. There was a reception at the Grand Imperial Hotel hosted by Don Stott and the Republican Party. I was Mayor then, and President of the Chamber of Commerce. (The man in the sunglasses in back, on the right, is a young Wiley Carmack, today owner of Outdoor World on Greene Street.

Gerald Swanson collection

even worse, saying the truth. And, sometimes the truth hurts. People don't like to hear the truth. Anytime you deal with money and personalities and projects, it's a tough combination. People get 'em all mixed up, tend to forget that if you don't get the projects done, if you don't have the right people working together to get things done, then you'd better have the right financing. It takes money to make money. It takes know-how and common sense. That's still true today, isn't it? People have a hard time working together, getting past their own personal agendas to accomplish something.

Chamber of Commerce—Money was also the issue, or the lack of it here, where I served as president for ten years. When I took over, we were still meeting at City Hall once a month, up in the old firemen's hall. I had a secretary and a treasurer, that's all. We wrote our own brochures, 'cause we didn't have anyone to write them

1977. Performing in "Carousel" with members of the Silverton Community Theater at the Bijou Theater, Grand Imperial Hotel. That's Mike Grimes on the far left, with Rick Adesso and Jim Alabashe. The guy on my right, with the dark beard, is Scotty Jackson. That's me in the wide-striped shirt.

Gerald Swanson collection

for us. We'd take them to a printer, but there was never enough money to do the job right. I'd appeal to the city and get $100. Then I'd hit up the county and get another $200. Chamber dues were $25 per year, and there was no distinction. The guy who owned the Grand Hotel paid the same as the guy who had a popsicle stand. And a lot of people didn't belong at all. (It's still not much different today.) So, to earn money, we had a lot of bake sales. If you wanted to talk to somebody at the chamber during the week, you couldn't; we all were working our own jobs.

Our first real functional Chamber of Commerce building was a caboose over at Potty Park (where the public restrooms are, on Blair Street). I got the old narrow gauge caboose from Lew Purcell and Fenrick Sutherland. We hauled it over there and reconditioned it. A friend of mine, a superintendent at the mine, sent a crew down with rails, ties and a work crew. They set out the rails and ties. The city hauled in the old caboose and put it on the rails for us. Volunteer labor painted it and made it very nice.

Herbert J. Schwartz, from Lebananon, Ohio, was our first manager. He could type faster with "hunt and peck" than most people could

1978. Delbert Smith entertains at Janet Swanson's graduation.

Gerald Swanson collection

on an electric typewriter. We put him in our new chamber building with our homemade brochures. He planted flowers outside and flew the American flag. I told old Herb, "I don't have any money to pay you." He asked if maybe by the end of the season we could pay $100 per month. To do that we had to come up with some scheme for making money.

SILVERTON

COLORADO

SILVERTON'S CENTENNIAL, 1874–1974

WHERE
YESTERDAY AND
TODAY MEET

That year was Silverton's one-hundreth birthday, our centennial. We planned all kinds of events to celebrate, but had to figure out how to pay for them. Now, we didn't have a big mailing list, and there was only one telephone line coming into the building. And the membership was small anyway.

So, Herb and I came up with a plan. He had a couple of hundred dollars and I had a couple hundred more. We ordered a big batch of wooden nickels with "Silverton Centennial" printed on them for merchants to sell out of their stores. The cost was $600 and we only had $400, so we went to the bank for a loan. The bank was up where the ice cream parlor is now. We signed a note for the chamber. We also bought Silverton Centennial glasses. The nickels cost two cents and we sold them for a quarter. The glasses cost a quarter and we sold them for two bucks. When the centennial was over, we had made a tremendous profit!

THANKS TO

GERALD SWANSON

OUR FEARLESS LEADER
DURING A GREAT
CENTENNIAL YEAR

1974

FROM
SILVERTON
CHAMBER OF COMMERCE

We also raised money for the first restoration of town hall (before it burned). Herb and I came up with the idea of having a "Coney Island Day." I asked Buzz Callaway to donate 200 to 300 weenies. Then I went to Charlie Schmalz (the Holsom Bread hauler) and got hot dog buns donated. An old Montrose distributing company donated ketchup, mustard and relish. Pepsi Cola gave us some premix. We set up at Potty Park, selling hot dogs and Pepsi Cola at ten cents apiece. Those hot dogs were gone in less than two hours! I went to the market, got some of our own, and we sold those too. It was fun, and we really cleaned up, made a bundle of money. Of course people around town, the restaurants, got mad, because we were basically giving away lunch! But that's the way it always is, isn't it?

We ran that chamber center out of that little caboose for four or five years. Herb got paid $300 at the end of the season for his three months. When he came back the next year, we really got cranked up. Herb was a natural. He looked like Buffalo Bill, with a white, pointed goatee and a long cloth coat.

He had one bad habit that got us in trouble, though. Herb would root for one certain thing, one certain business that he liked, and he wouldn't mention anybody else.

One day, the new manager of the Grand Imperial (a man from the Broadmoor in Colorado Springs owned it then) came down to the chamber. He asked Herb, "I'm new in town, where do you recommend for lunch?"

1974. Silverton's Centennial. Above: At the Chamber of Commerce "Potty Park" caboose with Herbert Schwartz. Below: With Alice the cow and my oldest daughter, Judy, representing Swanson's Market. Sign on Alice reads, "Fresh Milk, Diary Products."

Gerald Swanson collection

Herb had no idea who the guy was, and he sent him to the Bent Elbow, saying it was the best place in town to eat. (Which it was.)

The Grand Imperial guy said fine, then, pretty soon, he comes back with his assistant manager and makes a complaint. I had to send a letter of apology to the owner of the Broadmoor, but at the bottom of the letter, I put a Post Script: "I have to concur with Mr. Schwartz that the Bent Elbow is probably the best place to eat."

San Juan County Planning Commission—When I was on that commission (our first one), we were so busy trying to figure out what to plan. There were a lot of "experts" in town who had a liberal attitude. Allen Nossaman was a young man then, and many of us had differing opinions. I was kind of dumfounded. Fritz Klinke (today, owner of the Pickle Barrel and Smedley's Ice Cream) was on that commission with me. I think he still serves on it, so Fritz goes down in history

as the longest planning commission member in the state of Colorado. We were trying to help the City Council write new zoning, debating a green belt zone around Silverton. It was to be a buffer zone, so there wouldn't be building right into the sides of a cliff. Today, they're finding out it would be a good idea, although we never made it happen then. One of our biggest debates came up over a group from Arizona, which had purchased the bulk of the land south of town, down at the Wye. They wanted to put in a grandiose, tourist complex. Not surprisingly, the bulk of the business men on "main" street were against it. They didn't want the competition. (This is an attitude that still prevails with a number of people in Silverton, today.) That land is still sitting fallow today.

San Juan County Economic Development Board—I was also on the first board that they had around that same time. It was much the same story as it is today: what do we do to make Silverton more viable? It's like trying to reinvent the wheel. We still haven't found the right spokes to put on the hub. I advocate with my friend, James Burke, a local railroad buff, train photographer and co-publisher of the "All

1977 Hardrock Holidays Mining Contests. Left: Rose Rabb competes in the handmucking contest. (Today, Rose, married with children, still lives in Silverton, where she is a deputy at the San Juan Assessor's office.) Below: Billy Rhoades and his son Terry compete in drilling contest. (In the background is Louis Girodo and Jim Hook.) Below, left: Rick Ernst and Roy Andrean in team drilling. This team also won the same contest in 2001.

Gerald Swanson collection

1977. Judges for Hardrock Holidays celebration: Hal Slade, Herman Dalla, Frank Hitti, Gerald Swanson, Ernie Kuhlman, Bob Ward, Frank Montanetti.

Gerald Swanson collection

Aboard" magazine for the Durango and Silverton Railroad, that if we want to make Silverton a real destination, we reinstate gambling on Blair Street, in the style and fashion of the late 1800s. To participate, you have to dress in costume. There'd be none of this flashy neon stuff and slot machines with big lights on top. Instead, there'd be crap tables and poker tables with green tops, like the one still at the Miner's Tavern, and maybe a few old fashioned slots. We'd have honky-tonk piano players and maybe an act or two on stage, like in the old days. There'd be long bars with brass rails, saloon girls and bartenders with bowler hats. And spittoons around. We'd issue tobacco, but you couldn't smoke cigarettes.

1975. The growing Swanson family. Stela and David are in front with me. Claudia, Janet, Geraldine and Judy are in back.

Tommy Wipf

American Legion—One of my favorite jobs, and one of the longest lasting, was with the American Legion. I was adjutant of the Silverton Post for thirty-five years.

They talked me into joining in the mid-1950s, a month after I got out of the service. I was also District Commissioner of the American Legion for two years and District Chaplain for two years. When I joined, the bar was in the back room, and the present bar was a reading room and game room, with a pool table for the old Miner's Union. The bar served purely as a social outlet for members. We opened on Wednesday night for Rotary Club, Friday night for the Lions Club and Saturday for legionaries, their wives, friends and guests. The members took turns tending bar. There were fifteen guys on the bar committee. We all served one or two nights a month.

When we got the building, the roof leaked like a complete sieve. There were forty big metal flour buckets upstairs catching water. When a big snowstorm came, we'd go up there and shovel snow off the roof and from the attic. You could sit downstairs and hear water playing a tune in those buckets—plinky-plankey, plinky-plankey. Every spring, we held a roof patching party. That went on for twenty years. There was never enough money for repairs, so the auxiliary kept bailing us out with bake sales and other projects. We finally decided the South Hall (where they hold Bingo today) should belong to the auxiliary. Another way we made money was to rent out the hall for community functions, weddings and funerals.

The Legion limped along as a private club, until we hired Aunt Rena.

I remember one fellow in town, Thomas Savich, who was a charter member (he still spends his summers here) was a sort of guardian angel of the Legion. Tom was a reliable old boy. When we couldn't get anybody to fire the furnace—we all took turns— Tom would load the hopper, pull the clinkers and haul them outside. Tom was always there to help with the furnace, fill the beer coolers or shovel snow.

When Aunt Rena took over, and then Uncle Herman, the bar had already been moved up to its present location in front of the building. Business started booming. Then, out of sheer jealousy, some businessmen in town (bar owners) turned in the Legion for selling beer to non-members. They complained to the State Department of Revenue. There were constant hearings and battles. The place was closed down twice, so we finally went for a full liquor license and opened it up to the general

County services and Silverton Brass Band in front of Town Hall.   Gerald Swanson collection

1986. Receiving the "Citizen of the Year" award from the Chamber of Commerce. This was the first year this award was given, and I shared it with Ruth Ward, who was the San Juan County nurse at the time and owned the Blair Street Candle Shoppe. The banquet was held at the Bent Elbow. Presenting the award was George Chapman, then editor of the Silverton Standard.

Gerald Swanson collection

public as the Miner's Tavern in the American Legion.

Then A Theatre Group, which took over the upstairs, got $300,000 in grants and restoration funds. They used it to put on a new roof and shore up the building. The prime mover behind it was Marianne Fearn. Credit goes to her for keeping that building alive. She worked for practically nothing as director of A Theatre Group, bringing high-quality theater to the area. A couple of years ago Marianne won the (Colorado) Governor's Award for Excellence in the Arts.

That building, built by the AFL-CIO Miner's Union, on 11th and Greene, has been a community building from its inception. It also served as the prime mortuary during the Spanish Influenza of 1918 and was a great hardware and furniture store in the early 1900s (owned by a guy named Cooper). The building was also home to many fraternal organizations in town and had offices upstairs for groups like the Woodman of the World, International Order of Odd Fellows, IOFF, Forresters of America, Eagles Club (Tyrolen Trentini people), and it served as a meeting place for visiting Elks.

1977. With mother, Mary, at the market.
Gerald Swanson collection

Mary's 75th birthday. With my sister Jean and her husband Don Robinson, me and my wife Stela. The party was held at the French Bakery.

Gerald Swanson collection

Market headquarters

During the political years, I was also working with my mother, Mary, at the market—and later, running it. My mother hadn't much tolerance for my activities outside of the market, especially in the early days. "Gerald," she'd say, "You need to be in here cutting meat, not fooling around with all that stuff in town."

But things kept happening, like when the gunfights down by the Bent got out of hand and old Roy Landcaster, our city cop, came and got me, so we could put a stop to the shenanigans before somebody really got hurt! Or, when we had to clean the market out of hot dogs and Pepsi for the chamber's "Coney Island Day." There was always something going on, a meeting or a campaign that took up my time. I wore a lot of hats in those days. Of course, since I was mostly there, people could find me at the market, come there with their problems and questions. The market became a sort of personal headquarters during those years.

Because of my affiliation with the Republican Party, and many controversial elections, there were times when we lost a number of customers at the market. And, of course, my mother, who was a staunch Republican, used to raise hell with me for trying to mix politics and business. But, most of the time, those who got mad at me and quit coming to the store, would come back again anyway.

As I grew older, I began to realize that you really cannot mix business and

sentiment, rather politics or family. Any one who can be successful in that endeavor, needs to receive an additional award in heaven! *

1980. One of the last photos taken of the Dalla family, taken on Memorial Day on the front porch of my house in Silverton. Left-right, Fury Dalla, Rena Dalla Antonelli, Herman Dalla, Mary Dalla Swanson, Louis Dalla.

Gerald Swanson collection

1980. Geri Swanson, Alvine and Fury Dalla, Rena Antonelli, Stela Swanson, Mary Swanson, David Swanson, Herman Dala, Louis Dalla. Kneeling, Claudia Swanson, Celia Troglia, Joe Todeschi, Tommy Savich.

Gerald Swanson collection

✎ Ten ✎

After Market

Swanson's Market closed in 1988. I had thought about closing it years before—we had only one mine running, the Standard Metals Company (now Echo Bay). They started laying men off, little by little. I could see the handwriting on the wall. The town population was dropping, Greene Street Grocery was doing a good job and I was getting tired.

My mother was sick, off and on, and my wife started getting sick, too. It was time to close.

I had a number of other business interests in town over the years. I bought the old Club Cafe and Bar (where Fetch's is now) and was fixing it up. My mother and

Above: 1985, with my mother, Mary, at Swanson's Market. She was 83 years old and this was her last year at the market.

Left: 1987. The last year of Swanson's Market. We closed it the following year

Gerald Swanson
collection

47 years on Blair Street

by Chris Smith

Mary and Irwin Swanson purchased a building on Blair Street that had been a saloon. It had 16 foot ceilings, and both a back and front bar.

They opened a grocery store in the building on January 25, 1941, called Swanson's Market and on that first day sold $10.50 of food. There were loaves of bread available, milk from Ben Tomasi's dairy, a box of lettuce and beef.

Irwin Swanson was an excellent butcher. He borrowed $25 from his mother for a side of beef for the opening of his store. There was no refrigeration, so he hung it in the basement.

There were four other grocery stores in town at that time, and the meat did not sell as fast as they had hoped. In order to save it, the Swanson's stayed up all night and made Lugunega (Italian sausage) which Mary sold door to door the next day.

Irwin bought a used walk-in cooler next, and went to Rico for a load of sawdust to insulate it with. The cooler is still in operation at the store today.

As the new butcher's reputation spread, business picked up. Sales in January of that year were $60.17, and total sales for 1941 were $5,000.

The war started, and Irwin moved to Durango. Mary Swanson used the barter system to stock the store when she didn't have enough rationing stamps. She traded groceries with an Episcopalian minister named Hershey and he built shelves for

Later it was Ike Bausman who did the chore.

In 1955 Gerald Swanson finished college and his tour in the service, and came back to Silverton. He became the full time butcher, picking up the skill from his mother, meat salesmen, watching at the Calloway plant and just practising.

People told the Swansons that when the highway to Durango was paved, it would close their business, as folks would go out of town to buy their groceries. But it didn't happen. Business increased, and was especially profitable during a 10 year stretch in the 1970s when Swanson's was the only grocery store in town.

Hard work never bothered Mary Swanson, whose mother died when she was 16, and she not only raised her brothers and sisters, but ran the family boarding house. She then continued her ethic of hard work, conserving and saving money through the years at Swanson's Market, supporting her family alone.

Gerald remembers she never turned down anyone for credit, especially those with children. The uncollected credit over 47 years "could buy a fleet of Cadillacs" he says. He estimates it to be close to $50,000 or $60,000.

Mary also loaned the town of Silverton $2,800 to buy a dump truck in 1945, according to Gerald. She helped the town through rough times by holding the town's warrants until they could pay them, in order to pay salaries of town employees.

The closing of Swanson's

Hershey and he built shelves for her.

Mary had a son, Gerald, who was 11 at the time, and a daughter, Jean, who was 9 years old. Gerald remembers helping his mother package bulk food into smaller units, such as laundry soap, in the evenings. The family lived behind the store, and upstairs.

Every week Mary drove to Delta in a 1939 Chevrolet to buy meat for the store. Meat at Swanson's Market still comes from Delta, from Calloway Meats, for the last 30 years. In those days Caroline Tookey's father, Charlie Person would come down to the store at 5:30 a.m. to cut the meat.

The closing of Swanson's market marks the end of an era, a Silverton tradition representing a way of life that is one of the attractions of this small town. Mary Swanson, although, forced to stop working three years ago due to ill health, will be remembered for the 44 years she spent working in the store.

This article appeared in the Silverton Standard and Miner *in 1988 when the store closed.*

Gerald Swanson collection

We had quite a party when the store closed! Left: Al Holman, myself and Uncle Herman.
Bottom left: Al Homann and Lorenzo Groff, who owned Tyrolean Liquors for 25 years.
Below: Stela and me.

Gerald Swanson collection

David, Geri and I visited Stela's mother in San Francisco for her 95th birthday.

Gerald Swanson collection

I planned to have a restaurant there. But it cost too much to fix it right, so I sold it. I also owned the building next door and had it fixed up as a soda fountain and notion store. I leased that to the Grand Imperial people for three years, then sold it to the Darnell Zanoni family. They ran "The Parlor" (an ice cream parlor) in there, and it was a good one.

But, when I closed the store, I wasn't sure what I was going to do. My mother had died two years before—she was eighty-seven. My wife, Stela, had passed away two years later. It was a sad time.

Before we closed, since I knew I wouldn't be in the grocery business anymore, I tried to get all the old credit accounts cleared up. When I added up all the past due accounts, including the people who refused to pay and the accounts my mother and I had carried over the years, the total came to well over one hundred thousand dollars! Some of those bills went back forty years or more.

From groceries to gifts

We had a big sale and sold everything in the store at fifty percent off. Grocery store mark-up wasn't very good those days, any-way. You were lucky if you got twenty percent over cost. I sold the

The Town Hall burned in 1992 because of a short in a heat tape that smoldered and caught the roof on fire.

Silverton Town photo

balance of our inventory to Steve Smith at Greene Street Grocery, sold all the refrigerator cases, then left the building for the winter. Stela wasn't feeling so well then. In the spring, we opened a gift shop, "Swanees," where we sold the usual souvenirs, tee shirts and knick knacks. All of which I hated, so I opened a little

antique store where the little sluice building is now. I started selling off my mother's old antique furniture, taking it out of the upstairs, and I did very well at that. By then, Stela had passed away, so my daughter Geri managed the gift shop, while I managed the antique store. Then, I started running out of stuff to sell, and since I didn't want to run all over the country buying antiques, I turned the shop into a candy store, "Swanee's Sweets." I ran that three or four years, until too many other stores started putting in bulk candy.

Nancy Swanson
Gerald Swanson collection

Nancy and the Dallavalle Inn

Geri went back to teaching and I had decided to get out of the gift shop business, which I had never liked. It was about that time I met Nancy Downs. After we had dated for awhile, we got married right here in Silverton at St. Patrick's Catholic Church. Father Nathaniel Fosage performed the ceremony. Afterward we had a great wedding reception at the newly restored Town Hall. We rode to the reception in a horse and carriage.

© Kathryn Retzler

Left: Nancy and I, wedding photo.   (Tommy Wipf)
Below: Me and the boys, Carl Longstrom (his picture is also in my fourth grade birthday party in Durango, page 18), Thomas Savich and Don Robinson (in front).
Below: Wedding reception, Town Hall.

You couldn't tell who was having more fun, me or my newly-acquired grandkids. At Town Hall, we were met by Silverton's famous Brass Band. There we had a reception with all our friends and combined families. It was quite an event!

As for the old grocery-gift shop-candy store, we decided to remodel the building and turn it into a bed and breakfast. Nancy has a background in the restaurant business and catering, and she had always wanted to do a B&B.

It looked like a romantic idea at the time. I had a lot of family mementos, photographs, furnishings, antique and stuff; so, we made the place into an historic family museum. We named the rooms after my grandparents, Giovanni and Domenica, and Mary, my mother. We also have a Brass Band/Carousel room, the School room and

Room 7, "Domenica."

Kathryn Retzler

the Heritage room, with pictures of my uncles. All together there are seven rooms. The hallway is decorated with Silverton history and family history, Tyrolean (Austria-Italy) history—a tribute to my ancestors who came here from the Tyrol. My grandparents, the Dallavalles, are indicative of the many Tyrolean people who came here to work in the mines and businesses: men like my grandfather who had the John Dalla Bottling Plant (later called the Orella Bottling Works, and now the Crewel Elephant, a women's clothing shop), where he bottled soda pop and seltzer water. We named the B&B the Villa Dallavalle, after my grandparents.

Next door, in the vacant lot on the corner, we've put in Swanee's Sluice, "the cleanest mining sluice in the San Juans." It's fun for kids of all ages, and people coming in from the train often bring their kids over to sluice for treasure!

Full circle back—to old friends

Closing the store was traumatic, because I was raised in it. That building was my boy-

2002. Geri Swanson helps nephew Kelly Noon (son of her sister, Judy Noon) and Nancy's grandson, Bryson Thomas, sluice for treasure.

Kathryn Retzler

hood home as well as our family business. During all those years, it had been a gathering place for family and friends, customers and people from town. It was a place where friends stopped by to visit. Turning it into the Villa Dallavalle helped keep it a meeting place. The Dallavalle is a fine place to sit with guests and friends and share one of Nancy's wonderful breakfasts or a glass of good red wine in the evening along with a story or two of the old times. Old friends still come by every summer to tease me about buying good cheese, good meat. The other day, somebody came in who was a student of my Uncle Fury, who taught at the Silverton school for sixteen years.

We still have the old meat locker my father built—used today for storage, and the shelves on the side wall which used to hold groceries. Now they hold some of

Pat Swonger, I and John Ross at the Miner's.
Gerald Swanson collection

those family mementos. And I'm still involved in lots of things in the town, like I have always been—I'm on the board for A Theatre Group and I'm a lifetime member of the American Legion Post 14, for which I still do some public speaking. I don't get involved in politics anymore, at least not officially.

Nancy and I help host the Trentini gathering when it meets here in Silverton, and last year we went to the gathering in Trentino, Italy. The Trentini gathering is held here in Silverton every other year.

Even though I spent close to forty years in the market with my mother, which seems like a long time, you might conclude that I received a great education from a small town, and I am still learning more from old friends and acquaintances.

You can still get that education, that feeling of being part of a close, small community here in Silverton, and if you work at it, you can survive economically (although it's not always easy, especially not now).

We spent many years here when the times were tough. I can remember when we had not one mine running, after Standard Metal stopped. And, we didn't have the social welfare network and grants back then like we do now. The only thing we had was determination and faith in one another.

So it was tough, but we stuck together and we stuck it out.

The economy looked bleak again there for awhile, but more and more businesses are moving to town now. Sales tax revenues are up. More homes

Nancy and I help host the Trentini gathering when it is held in Silverton.
Kathryn Retzler

are being built and more people are moving here. Looking ahead, I do think the future of Silverton is going to be great. Silverton is a special place to live.

During the winter months, Nancy and I do a little traveling around the world, and inbetween trips, we winter in Texas. But no matter where we go or how far we travel, Silverton will always be my home. ✱

©James Burke

᠕ Index ᠕ Names

✄ Index ⋙
Businesses/Places

Index
Photograph Credits

Burke, Gerald Swanson collection; page 66, Kathryn Retzler; page 67, Gerald Swanson collection; page 68, Courtesy John Marshall with Zeke Zanoni, *Mining the Hardrock*; page 69, Allan Bird, T*hen and Now*; page 71-73, Gerald Swanson collection.

Chapter 5, page 75-76, Silverton School photo; page 81-86, Gerald Swanson collection; page 87, McNulty, Gerald Swanson collection; page 88-94, Gerald Swanson collection; page 95, Don Stott; page 96-101, Gerald Swanson collection.

Chapter 6, pages 102-106, Gerald Swanson collection.

Chapter 7, page 108-110, Gerald Swanson collection; page 111, James Burke, Gerald Swanson collection; page 112, Gerald Swanson collection; page 113, San Juan County Historical Society; page 114, Courtesy Grand Imperial Hotel, Kathryn Retzler; page 115, Gerald Swanson collection; page 116-117, Gerald Swanson collection; page 118, Kathryn Retzler; page 119, Gerald Swanson collection; page 120, Gerald Swanson collection, Kathryn Retzler; page 121, Gerald Swanson collection; page 122, San Juan County Historical Society; page 125-128, Gerald Swanson collection.

Chapter 8, page 129, Gerald Swanson collection; page 130, Tommy Wipf, Gerald Swanson collection; page 131-134, Gerald Swanson collection.

Chapter 9, page 135-142, Gerald Swanson collection; page 143, Gerald Swanson collection, San Juan County Historical Society; page 144-151, Gerald Swanson collection; page 152, Tommy Wipf; page 153-156, Gerald Swanson collection.

Chapter 10, page 157, Gerald Swanson collection; page 158, *Silverton Standard* article, Gerald Swanson collection; page 159, Gerald Swanson collection; page 160, Silverton Town photo, Gerald Swanson collection; page 161, Gerald Swanson collection, Kathryn Retzler; page 162, Tommy Wipf, Gerald Swanson collection; page 163, Kathryn Retzler; page 164, Gerald Swanson collection, Kathryn Retzler; page 165, James Burke.